lazy days and ducks on the waterside

cool canals
Pub days out (Britain)

Phillippa Greenwood and Martine O'Callaghan

Published March 2010 by
Coolcanals Guides
128 Newtown Road
Malvern, Worcestershire
WR14 1PF
info@coolcanalsguides.com
www.coolcanalsguides.com

OUR THANKS

A huge thanks to everyone who supported us
while we were making this guidebook,
especially our families and Tufty the boat cat.

Thanks also to those who have absolutely
nothing to do with the making of this
guidebook, but who help to keep Britain's
waterways open for everyone to enjoy: The
Waterways Trust, Inland Waterways Association,
Waterway Recovery Group, The Horseboating
Society, British Waterways, all local Canal
Societies, Trusts and Associations, and all
the stalwart volunteers with their enthusiam.

OUR ETHICS & THE ENVIRONMENT

We want to inspire visitors to keep using
their waterways and help Britain's canals
stay alive. At the same time, we never
knowingly support any business or activity
not in keeping with the community, culture
and traditions that make our canals special.

Because we care about the whole earth as
well as the waterways, we 'think' green
throughout every part of the process of
making our guides: from using Ecotricity in
our office and never driving if we can walk,
to choosing eco award-winning UK printers.

Printed and bound in the UK by
Butler Tanner & Dennis, Frome, Somerset

Cool Canals is printed using 100% vegetable-based
inks on Condat Silk FSC paper, produced from
100% Elemental Chlorine Free (EFC) pulp that is
fully recyclable. It has a Forest Stewardship
Council (FSC) certification and is fully manufactured
on one site by Condat in France, an ISO14001
accredited company. All FSC certified papers are
produced by companies who support well-managed
forestry schemes which in turn actively plant and
replace trees that are cut down for pulp, typically
planting more trees than are harvested. Butler
Tanner and Dennis are also fully ISO14001 accredited
and, by both printing and binding on one site,
dramatically reduce their impact on the environment.

Introduction to canals

Don't be fooled by the idyllic tranquillity. Canals are extreme destinations, with high aqueducts and tumbling lock flights linking urban landscapes to real countryside.

The blunt reality is that the canals were built over 200 years ago by the slavery of navvies for the profits of industrialisation. Great engineers such as Brindley and Telford created essential transport routes for entrepreneurs including Salt, Cadbury and Wedgwood in an era when the booming British manufacturing industry was dominating world economics. Raw materials and products from coal to pottery were carried by horse-drawn narrowboats along motorways of the time.

Canals stood for the status of material power and the new urbanism. Created for speed, canals now ironically offer space in which to slow down and escape from the very urban success they helped build. History probably wouldn't mind the twist of fate.

Canalmania ended when railways stole their trade and led to an era of neglect when canals were thought of as little more than stinking ditches. Now, loved again, they've become places to go for holidays and leisure - yet the battle for survival always burns beneath the surface.

The tradition of canal pubs

Even before the canals were built, pubs were at the heart of canal life. Meetings between engineers, financiers, landowners and other interested parties would have taken place in the Assembly Room of an inn. Once the project was approved with an Act of Parliament, the canal company could start building the canal (and more pubs!). Then it was the turn of navvies and boatmen to cement a long tradition of canalside drinking and socialising.

What's special about canalside pubs?

Bar stools are more than just bar stools in a canal pub: most have propped generations of boatmen's tales. The hum of pub chatter across the water once made working life bearable for the Victorian boatman; and now it makes a leisure-seeker's day with conversations swinging from the marvels and mishaps of modern-day boating. Waterways pubs make you want to sit with a pint in your hand, soak up the atmosphere and forget any ideas of rushing off.

The Lock, the Navigation, the Boat - their names are living history and behind every canal pub's front door, there usually lies the waterways tradition of a warm welcome, and a good pint! Some waterside pubs predate the canals, a few are new, but many were built for the navvies and boatmen who first worked on the canals during the heady years of the Industrial Revolution. Ale was safer to drink than filthy water, so jugs of ale kept thirsty workers pleasurably quenched. Drunkenness was mandatory and raucous evenings of ale and song a matter of life.

It's hard to imagine the idyllic pubs tucked on today's quiet waterways were once the equivalent of motorway pubs. From a time before the engine, with horse-towed boats, waterways made the fastest trade routes. Waterways times and fortunes may have changed, yet still, after over 200 years, real ale is served with a culture of no frills or prejudice, whether you're a navvie, an entrepreneur, a landowner, a boater, an adventurer or just a Coolcanals guide writer.

Canalside pubs unwittingly facilitate shoulder-rubbing where differences and hierarchies are magically diluted by the balm of water. On our towpath travels, we never doubted the welcome from strangers at the next pub-stop. Thankfully, canalside pub manners seem to have a will of their own that defies modernity.

Not just another pub guide

This isn't just another fact-packed pub book. It's an impassioned sketch with frank observations that tells you the things that matter when you're looking for somewhere special to go for a good pub day out.

'Cool canals Pub Days Out' is an invitation to enjoy lazy days out discovering Britain's fascinating canals, and enjoying some of the best waterside pubs we've found. Every pub in this guide has been handpicked, not only for its own 'pubby' virtues, but also for its location near some very special waterways highlights - that's anything from a good location for gongoozling (watching boating activities) to an idyllic pub-stroll with extraordinary waterways sightseeing, or perhaps a short boat trip and even a bit of souvenir shopping.

We give the travel essentials whether you arrive by car, boat, train, bike, boot or bus and all the important info you need to plan your day out. We tell you about waterways features not to miss and give our own spiked and honest account of each pub day out we've selected.

In winter this guidebook steers you to cosy open fires inside characterful canal pubs where you can snuggle up and forget the world. And in summer, stretch out in the great waterways outdoors, lolling in waterside beer gardens watching narrowboats drift by.

We hope these great pub days out along Britain's canals will inspire you to take time for long lazy lunches on the waterside, enjoying locally brewed ales and ciders, and soaking up the slow charms of some very special canalside pubs. (We're totally independent and nobody has bribed us with a free pint to be included in this guidebook. We've simply loved each pub day out for its own virtues.)

How this book happened...
'THE GREAT CANAL WALK'

We've travelled the canals by narrowboat and walked the towpaths all across Britain, coast to coast and end to end from Cornwall to Scotland.

Our journey has followed the water roads through the Welsh mountains, over the Pennines, across the Peak District, the Cotswolds, along the Great Glen Way, into the Lake District and even secretly sidled through London by the back door.

We've already collected sand in our boots on the Bude Canal, felt wind in our faces on the Caledonian and kept our bellies warmed in some characterful canalside pubs along the way... And our mission is to track down every canal in Britain.

When we set off, just for fun, on our slow end-to-end towpath walk from the Bude Canal in Cornwall to the Caledonian Canal in Scotland, we didn't have a pub guidebook in mind. But after strolling only a few water miles we'd already discovered that pubs are not only part of the bricks and mortar of canal heritage, they're also the beating heart of canal culture.

Typically we reach a canalside pub every few miles, and throughout our 2,000 mile or so trek, that adds up to a lot of great pubs. Some more memorable than others, but all unique with that indefinable spirit of the waterways.

Canalside pubs are a sociable place for water travellers: it's where boaters gather at the end of a day's cruising, it's a watering hole for cyclists, a meeting place for locals, a hub for the canal community - and a chance for walkers like us to pull off our boots and take time over a pint.

Since nothing hurries on the waterways, neither should we. Our pleasure continues to unravel with the unbridled task of lingering over glassfuls of good ale, swilled in good company (mostly). Some remarkable canal-days allowed this guidebook to write itself.

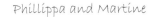

Phillippa and Martine

What we think makes a good pub

The best canal pubs are those which have survived unspoilt by progress, nurturing the same spirit of community that makes every water traveller welcome. A good landlord or landlady's welcome should be as warm to strangers as it is to regulars (and we have a hunch that a pub is happiest when dogs are welcomed too, even if they might shed a hair on the carpet).

The smartest settees won't automatically impress us. And a folded beer-mat wedging a wobbly table leg doesn't upset us either; it might simply signal the beautiful ordinariness of a pub without fake charms. Of course nobody likes sticky tables, or rock-hard globs of decayed ketchup smeared on the exterior of a white porcelain salt-cellar, but out-of-fashion décor never harmed a soul.

We try to avoid pubs with vulgar themes, scowling bar staff that avoid eye contact, grizzly cliques, over-blown-up sports TV, or anonymous music systems that inflict the second run round of the same passion-free, middle-of-the-road medley.

The role of food in a bar is a contentious debate between pub purists and new trends. We say real ale and real food go well enough together, but we prefer pubs that don't pre-lay empty tables with knives and forks and make those who only want a drink feel second class. We think reserving a table is something you should do in a restaurant, not a pub. Coach parties of eaters, clattering cutlery and fumes from the carvery are better confined to cafeterias.

If a few pubs in this guide serve sublime platters of gastro snobbery, many more won't. Our concern is not the frills or fashions of food and whether the beef and mash should come with jus or be smothered in gravy. If a pub is special for its own reason, we don't mind if the chalk board offers us Halloumi cheese on ciabatta, or if we just have to point to the cling-wrapped bap we fancy from the stash stacked on a plate behind the bar.

The pubs we pick are those that best capture something special about canals and offer a good day out - a great waterways atmosphere, historic architecture, interesting quirks of some sort, decoration with unusual canalia, seating with good gongoozling, taps that pull exceptional real ale brewed locally, real food, real fires, or simply the indefinable pleasure of cosy corners and hideaways.

We've travelled the canals all the way from Cornwall to Scotland and brought memories back of not only some very special waterways pubs, but also some fascinating people and amazing canal places... and, we admit, affirmed a spectacular passion for good beer too.

We've admired some pubs that know how to treat children with respect and ask for it back, and we've been impressed by others that aren't afraid to ignore the giant pub chain-gang mentality. Inevitably, it was a long list we had to whittle down to choose the best pub days out to fit into this book.

There are others, of course.

THE PUBS

* 7 Wonders of the Waterways

Contents

Introduction to canals 6

What's special about canalside pubs? 7

Not just another pub guide 9

How this book happened 10

What we think makes a good pub 12

Map & contents 14

The Pubs -

1 Boat Inn - Northamptonshire 17

2 Double Locks - Devon 27

3 Bottle & Glass - West Midlands 39

4 Tunnel End Inn - West Yorkshire 49

5 Fleur de Lys - Warwickshire 61

6 Clock Warehouse - Derbyshire 71

7 Tap & Spile - Birmingham 83

8 Star Inn - Wales 93

9 Foxton Locks Inn - Leicestershire 105

10 Shroppie Fly - Cheshire 115

11 The Turf - Devon 127

12 Telford Inn - Wales 137

13 Navigation Inn - Derbyshire 149

14 The Weighbridge - Worcestershire 159

15 Swan Inn - Staffordshire 171

16 Ring O' Bells - Cheshire 181

17 George Inn - North East Somerset 193

18 Admiral Nelson - Northamptonshire 203

19 Waterside beer festival 215

20 Canalside brewery 223

More canalside breweries 232

Real ale rantings 234

Real ale facts 237

101 more waterways pubs 238

Gone gongoozling 242

Things to look out for 244

7 Wonders of the Waterways 248

Waterways who's who 249

Useful info 250

Glossary 252

About Coolcanals Guides 254

Boat Inn
Grand Union Canal

Most pub days out are easy to plan, but head for the Boat Inn at Stoke Bruerne and your day will organise itself: this pub is in a waterways hub.

Often villages, towns and cities miss the chance to tell anyone where their canal is, but Stoke Bruerne isn't that daft. If you arrive by road, signposts clearly invite you to their canal.

If you wander down to the canal at the heart of Stoke Bruerne village on a warm summer's day, you'll step into a perfect olde English scene. A holiday picture not dissimilar to a rustic coastal cove, except instead of Aran-wrapped seafaring fishermen standing around and nattering amongst themselves, it's pot-bellied boatmen from narrowboats with their bandana-clad boat dogs. Non-boating visitors stand out from the locals because of their cameras and ice creams - and dogs outnumber everyone.

The Boat Inn knows its worth, grabbing eyes from the canalside with its thatched roof. Inside, an interesting bunch of rooms await, but the two tiny bar rooms are by far the most evocative. Planked seats tuck into stonework, bar stools wobble on old stone-flagged floors, and the genuinely battered chequered tiles are a joy.

Sit in here and you're going to chat to someone you didn't arrive with. Look out for the nifty trick of the old Border collie that can catch Frisbee beer-mats in the bar. Have a go at the bar game of Northants skittles or read the history of the pub mounted on the walls.

"Stand and have a drink on me" says a tile on the floor under your feet as you queue at the bar: 'Jack 1924-2008'. Such is the character of this ancient pub, that Jack, the former landlord, still makes his warm presence felt. The pub is currently being run by the fourth generation of the Woodward family who took over the pub in 1877.

There's the promise of relaxing real fires and indoor canal chat in winter and in summer, sit outside to watch passing boats, old boaters in hats, children playing, dogs, and weekend waitresses shuttling earnestly.

At busy times you'll be lucky to snatch a table on the water's edge at the front of the pub, but inside has bags of space with a lounge and bistro staged on seemingly endless levels in the newer extended (albeit less appealing) eating areas of the pub.

The pub also has a separate restaurant and cocktail bar housed in a timber and stone 'barn style' extension. There's even a small shop selling essentials to passing boaters and ice creams to day-trippers.

The beer is good and so is the food and the character of this canalside pub speaks for itself. The 'olde' England package is completed by the Rose & Castle Morris dancers, based at the Boat Inn, who can frequently be caught jangling folkishly on the canal side.

Make a day of it...

National Waterways Museum - Stoke Bruerne

The National Waterways Museum is split into three sites: Stoke Bruerne, Gloucester Docks & Ellesmere Port. Stoke Bruerne Museum is opposite the pub and housed upstairs, with displays of models, artefacts, videos and old photographs telling stories of the 'cut' covering two centuries.

The shop at ground level is packed with everything from museum chutney, canal books, traditional canal art, decorated wooden spoons, plastic ducks and pens - to the unrelated trivia that we all get the urge to buy for unknown reasons when we're out for a day.

There's also the fun of the WOW (Wild over Waterways) Trail for children, with a hunt inside the museum and along the canal. It's popular and, on the day we visited, kids armed with paper, pencils and pointing fingers were trotting around the canalside on a mission.

National Waterways Museum
Wheelchair access ground floor only.
Apr - Oct Daily 1000 - 1700. Nov - Mar Wed - Fri 1100 - 1500, Sat - Sun 1100 - 1600.
T:01604 862229 www.nwm.org.uk

The Toll House

In the 18th century, the Toll House was used to collect tariffs payable from the working narrowboats laden with cargo. (In 1975 it was offered as a retirement cottage to boaters Fred and Ivy Fielding who were Salvation Army missionaries.

Sister Mary Ward

One of the canalside cottages used to be the home of Sister Mary Ward. Despite having no official training, she became the acting nurse and doctor to working boat families for over fifty years. Proud and independent boaters trusted her, and would wait until they could get to Stoke Bruerne to be treated.

Stoke Bruerne Locks

On busy weekends, any boaters daring to cruise through Stoke Bruerne Top Lock in full view of the pub will have to brace themselves for wasps of onlookers. Despite its popularity with gongoozlers, the rest of the lock flight is not the prettiest on Britain's canal networks; but if you're willing to stretch further than a stroll, the views beyond open out with Northampton's best rural charm.

Towpath amble

It's only a short stroll from the pub to the entrance of Blisworth Tunnel, third longest on the canal network. Along the way you pass the old stables used for working boat horses, an old tug store and a segment of rebuilt tunnel section.

Seats are conveniently positioned for gongoozlers by a winding hole (where boats that don't fancy the dark tunnel can turn around).
Sit on the wall by the tunnel and if you hear chugging, a boat may be on its way – but sound carries a long way over water, so you may have to wait in 'canal time'.

Boat trip

The Boat Inn runs boat trips in its own narrowboat, the 'Indian Chief'. The standard 25-minute trip is from the pub to the tunnel and back, and the boat is also available for private parties or celebrations with extended cruises beyond the tunnel.

Pub nitty-gritty

The Boat Inn
Stoke Bruerne
Nr. Towcester
Northamptonshire
NN12 7SB
T:01604 862428
www.boatinn.co.uk

Opening hours

All year, daily 0930 - 2300 (Sun to 2230).

Food

Served all day. Good choice of reasonably priced bar food from hot baguettes to pan-fried Seabass, while the restaurant offers a wider choice and daily special lunches. Child-friendly food portions. Veggie options.

Drink

Freehouse.

Permanent ales: Local brewery Frog Island Bitter, Marstons Pedigree & Old Empire, Jennings Cumberland, Wychwood Hobgoblin.

Guest ales: Rotating basis.

Other drinks: Thatchers Traditional Hand Pull Cider and Hoegaarden on tap. Speciality coffees.

Other essentials

Dog-friendly

Wheelchair access (although tricky through the older bars).

Real fires

The pub is also involved with the annual boat gathering in June, the Stoke Bruerne Village at War weekend in October and other events throughout the year.

GONGOOZLING

If you can manage to get one of the outside tables, gongoozling opportunities are endless. Stoke Bruerne Top Lock is just by the pub and is busy with boats most of the season, and the pub's own trip boat moors right in front of the tables.

TIP

Turn up any Wednesday evening to see the Rose & Castle Morris dancers practising their routines (& having a beer or two!). And on St. George's Day, up to 12 Morris sides get together here.

And for afternoon tea...

The Museum's Waterside Café has friendly staff, good coffee and a view of the water.

Hours as Museum. Wheelchair access.

THE DAY IN A NUTSHELL

Quintessential English canal village.

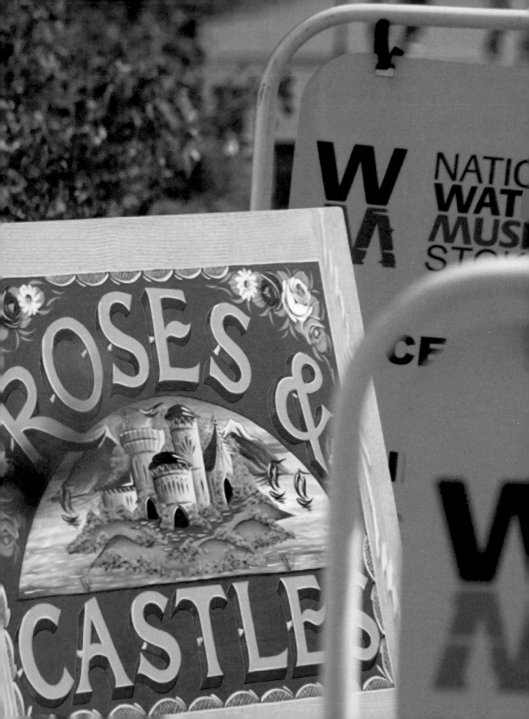

Location

OS Grid ref: SP743498

Canal: Grand Union Canal, by Stoke Bruerne Top Lock

OS Explorer Map: 207

How to get there

By train
Nearest train station is Northampton
National Rail Enquiries T:08457 484950

By bus
Traveline T:0871 2002233

By car
Parking at the pub or roadside and when busy, the village takes over a field as a car park.

By boat
Stoke Bruerne Boat Company
Day boat hire, skippered cruise and trip boat.
T:07966 503609 www.stokebruerneboats.co.uk

'Indian Chief'
Trip boat run by the Boat Inn.
T:01604 862428 www.boatinn.co.uk

Moorings
There are some moorings outside the pub and plenty of 48-hour moorings on the opposite side of the canal, most of the way from Stoke Bruerne Museum to Blisworth Tunnel.

Local Tourist info

Explore Northamptonshire
T:01604 609 393
www.explorenorthamptonshire.co.uk

Stoke Bruerne town website
www.stokebruerne.org.uk

Double Locks
Exeter Ship Canal

A boldly painted pub sign beckons with attitude (and a hint of tautology) from a building that happens to overlook the double lock on Exeter's canal. It's only a mile and a bit from the busy canal quayside but far enough to be a great escape for a day.

Everything about this pub is calling discerning pub goers, and arriving is almost an act of pilgrimage as walkers, cyclists and canoeists approach in union. You could almost feel out of place if you arrived by car - but don't worry, nobody would make you less welcome if you did. Anyway, it really doesn't matter how you get here, just get here if you can; this is one of our favourite pubs anywhere on Britain's canals.

The Exeter Ship Canal is far too sea-bound for flat-bottomed narrowboats, so you won't see quaintly painted roses and castles on the decks of boats round here. The Double Locks has a different character to most canalside pubs. It reeks of seafaring history, but its charm is that it never gets bogged down with nostalgia. It's too busy enjoying the great waterways outdoors: bikes, paddles and dog leads prop every bench and ledge.

Several rooms greet you inside. Raw wooden tables are allowed to breathe without nasty 'wipe clean' overcoats stifling their spirit. Canoes hang from the ceiling, rustic panelling hugs the walls and husky music flows into the atmosphere. Blackboards tempt you with intriguing options such as Russian Cabbage Soup, and the menu is ample with ethical free-range choices too.

Every way the eye explores in the bar is fascinatingly ordinary and extraordinary. Look up to see a quirky cartoon mural, then look down and you'll see scuffed sandals queuing to be served. And every so often next to them, you spot the even hairier legs of dogs queuing for their free doggie treats from a tub on the bar. Under 18s can't go in the bar, but the rule is waived for dogs. You don't have to be here long to grasp that this pub's claim to be dog friendly isn't half pint. Dog leads and water bowls are as natural as beer-mats and bar stools. Cosy fires are for sharing in winter and well-behaved dogs aren't forced to be shackled to your ankles. The garden is a social opportunity for all and there's swimming too. Every year they even throw a dog show.

Both children and dogs appear beside themselves with contentment. It's a happy pub – effortlessly calm with pervading activity. Kids visibly enjoy this fulfilling non-plastic ambience without the bore of over-contrived screeching that too frequently goes with the 'child friendly' label. There's a subtle play area and a convivial volleyball net that the kids might have to share with grown-ups.

On summer weekends, barbeques and an outside bar add to the garden experience, all mingled with green grass, trees for company and water to watch. It's a relaxed pub that understands the freedom of the waterways outdoors and does something liberating to most who spend time here. Everything adds up to make this pub funky-cool; and best of all it seems genuinely unpretentious and believably honest. Seaside shabby, ruggedly well-used and blatantly well-loved.

Exmi
Dawl

2 🚲

Cou
Tops

🚲

EXE CYCLE
Double Loc
City centre

2 🚲

Make a day of it...

Not a canal purist's experience. It's more tamed river than canal, and how you get to the pub is the main part of your day out. Walk, bike or why not go by canoe?

By boot

The Exeter Ship Canal is part of the Exe Valley Way, a long-distance trail covering 50 miles northwards from Starcross to the village of Exford on Exmoor. Walking from Exeter, you can choose to walk on either side of the canal. Unusually, the Exeter has towpaths on both sides that once enabled two working horses at a time to pull large ships.

Trip boat

The trip boat 'Kingsley' sets off hourly from Exeter quayside to the Double Locks pub. Daily in June, July & August. Weekends & Bank hols only April, May & September.
T:07984 368442
www.exetercruises.com

By bike

The entire length of the canal is part of National Route 2 of the Sustrans National Cycle Network.
www.sustrans.org.uk

Canoe and bike hire

At Exeter's quayside, you can hire all types of bikes from mountain bikes to tandems and child bikes to trailers. Single and double kayaks, open Canadian canoes. Saddles & Paddles also stocks a range of bikes for sale, and is open daily all year.
T:01392 424241
www.saddlepaddle.co.uk

Canoe trips

Full or half day canoe trips along the Exeter Ship Canal including some basic bush craft lessons.
T:01395 200522
www.essential-adventure.co.uk

Boat trip to the canal end

The White Heather ferry runs three times a day from Double Lock to Turf Lock. It goes past the now disused Topsham Lock (where it's possible to catch another ferry across the estuary to Topsham) and drops you off just above Turf Lock at the canal end, next to Turf pub.
T:07806 554093

The Double Lock

The huge double lock was built in the late 1600s to replace the original trio of locks. It was so unusually large that small boats were carried round the lock on rail tracks to save the water, time and effort needed to fill the lock chamber.

Pub nitty-gritty

Double Locks
Canal Banks
Exeter
Devon
EX2 6LT
T:01392 256947
www.doublelocks.com

Opening hours

Mon - Fri 1100 - 2300 (Sat to midnight, Sun to 2230).

Food

Mon - Thu 1200 - 1430 & 1800 - 2100.
Fri, Sat 1200 - 2100, Sun 1200 - 1800.
Great choice of food from Young's pies to sandwiches & wraps. BBQ area in summer.
Free-range and veggie options.

Drink

Young's Brewery pub. Utterly satisfying ales.
Barrels row up as a backdrop to the already tempting array of taps at the bar.

Permanent ales: Young's Bitter, Young's Special.

Guest ales: Seasonal ales, eg Young's Winterwarmer. Others from local breweries include O'Hanlon's Yellowhammer, Otter Ale, St Austell Tribute, Branscombe Vale Branoc, Bays Gold.

Other drinks: Comprehensive wine list.

Other essentials

Dog-friendly

Wheelchair access

Real fires

GONGOOZLING

Gongoozling is a passive sport, but at the Double Locks pub, everyone in turn becomes part of the spectacle.

Sitting in the beer garden alongside the canal, you'll be gongoozling people as they arrive by bike or on foot, watching others drag their canoes in and out of the water, and dogs leaping about in the water.

TIP

You'll be spoiled for choice with the real ales. In the end, we went for O'Hanlon's Yellowhammer and St Austell's Tribute - delicious!

Live music on most Saturdays from April to September.

THE DAY IN A NUTSHELL

Big food, big ale, big lock.

Location

OS Grid ref: SX932900

Canal: Exeter Ship Canal, below the Double Lock

OS Explorer Map: 110/114

How to get there

By train
Exeter St Thomas, Exeter Central and Exeter St Davids.
National Rail Enquiries T:08457 484950

By bus
Traveline T:0871 2002233

By car
Car park near quayside (charge) or at the pub

By boat
Hourly cruises in 'Kingsley' from Exeter quayside to Double Locks pub. Daily June, July & August. Weekends & Bank hols only in April, May & September. Also available for private charter.
T:07984 368442 www.exetercruises.com

Moorings
Apart from 'Kingsley', most boats arriving at this pub are canoes. Places above and below the lock to climb out of the water, and to relaunch.

Local Tourist info

Quay House Visitor Centre
A free exhibition with displays of the history of Exeter's woollen industry and the canal.
Open Apr - Oct daily 1000 - 1700,
Nov - Mar Sat - Sun 1100 - 1600.
T:01392 271611 www.exeter.gov.uk

Exeter town website
www.exeter.gov.uk

Bottle & Glass
Dudley Canal

Liken a Lancastrian to a Yorkshireman if you dare, but never, never confuse a Blackcountryman with someone from Birmingham. Intellectuals can pontificate about similarities between the two regional dialects, but if they cor tell a Blackcountrymon from a Brummie, they'm saft.

The Black Country was the mule, the slave, the entrepreneur, the brains, the brawn and the absolute making of the Industrial Revolution over 200 years ago. The manufacturing industries that made Britain wealthy, thrived on the Black Country's local coal, iron ore and the imported labour of workers from England's impoverished agricultural land. Canals curl round almost every backyard in these parts and a Black Country child still grows up playing down by the 'cut'. But times have changed and progress has demolished yesterday's corner shop, community hall, cobbled streets and local pub with a proper snug - and the old skyline has been replaced with shopping mall fever.

The Black Country Living Museum is a dedicated stroke of genius that has saved ordinary, but historic, buildings and moved them to an open-air site along the Dudley Canal. Every brick in every building was numbered so that the reconstruction could be accurate. The museum says in its guide that it is 'Britain's friendliest open-air museum', and the minute you arrive you agree. The whole thing is a bit like walking in on a film set with friendly folk going about their daily business in period dress. The visitor becomes part of a living bubble of history.

The Bottle & Glass pub sits in prime location in the museum, as any good pub would have done in the heydey of the Victorian era. Interestingly, the Black Country is said to have more pubs per mile than anywhere in Britain. In its former life, the Bottle & Glass sat on the canalside by the Sixteen Locks (at lock 2) on the Stourbridge Canal, built around the same time as the canal in the late 1700s. The pub finally closed its doors in 1979, but was saved when it was given to the museum. Now, instead of pulling ale for miners, glass-cutters and working boatmen, the pub welcomes tourists.

Debbie, the landlady will pull you a pint with a ruby smile, and equally turf you out if you misbehave - but then she is over 200 years old, from an era when landladies kept a tight guard on their pub. Debbie is a mine of information and milks every story she can. She's likely to make you forget she's in role (in real life she's a music teacher) and if she's not introducing you to Dougie the stuffed duck-billed platypus (on a shelf over the bar), she'll be relaying tales of rattle-chested miners who used to sit on the hard wooden bench next to the fire, right where you're sitting.

The old mines and smog-ridden air gave the area its name, and messed with the lungs of the workers. Spitting was a way of life not a statement. This front bar is genuine 'spit and sawdust'. And to prove it, there's even sawdust on the floor. Spittoons are strategically positioned by the fire for those who couldn't spit as far as the fire, and the sawdust catches the rest.

The whole museum is an utterly fascinating day out and the cream on the top is that you get traditional Black Country real ale here too. And it's the right colour, with the right head, served at the right temperature. Ask for a lager at your peril.

PHILIP HAMISH MacDONALD WOOD
Licensed Victualler
& RETAILER OF SPIRITUOUS
LIQUORS
ALES, WINES, PORTER, CIDER
& TOBACCO
To be consumed on the Premises

DUDLEY

34

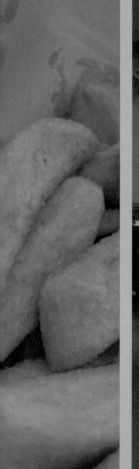

Make a day of it...

Explore the Museum

The Museum is a huge open-air site with over 40 historic buildings and exhibits to wander around.

The Houses

The museum is perfect permission to do the nosey thing - wander in and out of other people's houses, then have a peep round the back. You'll find pig sheds in the yard and interesting outdoor loos with torn bits of newspaper instead of tissue. Stoves keep the tiny front rooms as warm and cosy as a narrowboat cabin. Tables are covered in cloths, that cover cloths, that cover more cloths - and armchair arms get the same protective Victorian treatment too. The TV is missing, there's no road noise, and there's lots of stuff that your gran used to use.

The Chip Shop

In the Black Country, beer and chips just go together. Health and safety stops them wrapping the chips in newspaper now, but the Chip Shop claims to serve the best good old-fashioned fish and chips you can get anywhere. And who would argue.

The Workers' Institute

It's worth looking round the Workers' Institute, even if it's only to spare a moment in awe of the Cradley chainmakers. An exhibition room tells you about the audacious women of Cradley who dared to strike at work, and the shocking antics of Mary McArthur who helped them. Newspaper cuttings from the 1920s are on display with outrageous headlines about the chainmakers and their strike.

The Mine

The reason the area was called the Black Country! The mine shows that to be working class once meant 'working' to survive, and sometimes to your death. You get a guided walk (or stoop) with just a dim torch for comfort. As you go underground, it gets cold with only wretchedly damp air to breath in the dark. You could swear you can hear the sounds of life and death in the heavy silence. Model horses tell how they once pulled tons of coal along the shafts, and the ghosts of generations of miners talk about their miserable jobs and dangerous life expectancy. Clever props give you a few hair-raising surprises (but we won't tell and spoil it for you!).

The Indoor Exhibition

The indoor exhibition near the museum's entrance takes you through the history of the museum's buildings. There are large images, artefacts and interactive information screens. You can even have a go at legging through a tunnel on the model - hilarious fun!

Shire horses

The stable for the working shire horses is next door to the pub. If the horses are not in the stable, they will either be grazing in the field or down by the canal towing the boats.

Boat Trip into Dudley Tunnels

A spectacular network of canal routes burrow deep into dark limestone tunnels. Boat trips into the Tunnels are run by the Dudley Canal Trust, from the canal next to the Museum. The boats run daily every 15-30 minutes throughout the summer (Wed - Sun winter). In December, the Trust also run special Santa trips into the Tunnel.

Pub nitty-gritty

The Bottle & Glass
Black Country Living Museum
Tipton Road
Dudley
West Midlands
DY1 4SQ
T:0121 5579643
www.bclm.co.uk

Museum opening hours

Mar - Oct Daily 1000-1700.
Nov - Feb Wed-Sun 1000-1600.

Food

Food is served during the museum's opening hours. You won't get modern-fangled gastro food in the pub - you'll be lucky if you get a cheese and onion cob!

Within the museum site, there's the Café Bar, the Chip Shop, the Canalside Café or picnic areas to choose from. Veggie options.

Drink

Permanent ales: Good solid well-kept Black Country ales.

Other drinks: Some of the usual spirits, and a choice of soft drinks, bottled beers and cider.

Other essentials

Only guide dogs allowed.

Wheelchair access (although not into some of the museum's individual properties).

Children are not allowed in the front bar of the pub.

Real fires

GONGOOZLING

The pub has a small garden by the canal. You can't see the water but the living museum experience is the point of this pub.

TIP

During term-time, the Museum can get busy with large school parties (but they're not allowed in the bar, so it's still quiet in there).

The Museum Shop

Leave enough time at the end of the day to browse round the shop. It's heaving with Black Country mugs, books, sweets, even T-shirts scribed with a dictionary of Black Country lingo.

THE DAY IN A NUTSHELL

A fascinating peep into Black Country heritage and a pub with no music, no juke box, no noise at all. Just good old-fashioned chattering.

Location

OS Grid ref: **SO950915**

Canal: **Dudley Canal, near Dudley Tunnel**

OS Explorer Map: **219**

How to get there

By train
Nearest station is Dudley Port
National Rail Enquiries T:08457 484950

By bus
Traveline T:0871 2002233

By car
Museum car park

By boat
Trip boats into Dudley Tunnels & the Singing
Cavern, next to the Black Country Living
Museum. Boats run every 30 mins (every
15 mins at busy times). Wheelchair access.
Special trips also available.
Mar - Oct Daily 1000-1700. Jan, Feb, Nov
Wed - Sun 1000-1600. Dec Santa event only.
T:01384 236275 www.dudleycanaltrust.org.uk

Moorings
There's a water point on the canal just outside
the pub. Some short-term moorings opposite
and the other side of the road bridge.

Local Tourist info

Black Country and Dudley Tourist Info
T:0300 5552345 www.dudley.gov.uk
www.blackcountrytourism.co.uk

Heart of England website
www.visittheheart.co.uk

Dudley Canal Trust
Initially set up in 1963 to protect the tunnel, the
Trust now runs the boat trips, using the funds
raised to maintain the canal & its environment.
T:01384 236275 www.dudleycanaltrust.org.uk

Tunnel End Inn
Huddersfield Narrow Canal

If you're looking for a day out to wake up all the senses, then West Yorkshire is the place to go. Nothing happens by half measure and the landscape is allowed to be wild.

Head for Marsden Moor (part of the South Pennine Moors) on the edge of the National Trust Estate and the boundary of the Peak District National Park. Visitors around these parts can't help but hear the hormones of Heathcliff whistling in winds from the north, and only a fool could miss the passion of this place.

Marsden has a long tradition of non-complacency and history shows locals of the past were a feisty bunch with uprisings in their bones (from the Suffragette Movement to the Marsden Luddites). When the Huddersfield Narrow Canal arrived in the late 1700s, it brought the Industrial Revolution with it. For good or bad, that meant textile mills would be forever knitted into the area's history; but by a twist of industrial-fate the green landscape can now ask to be loved for its extreme natural beauty as well.

The canal melts into the moorland with its miraculous journey: 20 miles, 74 locks and 3 tunnels, from Dukinfield Junction (in the outskirts of

Manchester) all the way to Huddersfield.

When the Pennines got in the canal's way, it just tunnelled straight through, as if they weren't in the way at all! Standedge Tunnel is the longest, highest and deepest tunnel on Britain's canals. The navvies who built the Pennine waterways often risked their lives, knuckelling and shovelling underground in all seasons and the cruellest weather.

No one who arrives at the point where the canal disappears into the tunnel can pretend to be a passive voyeur - after you have marvelled in disbelief at the engineering feat that dug deep down into the dark hole, the destination sweeps you back up to its great outdoor surroundings.

The airy scene does its best to dazzle with the remoteness of moorland, but you're unlikely to be alone: the pub nearby brings locals out for a quick pint, and you might meet exhausted boaters there, envigorated walkers or high-energy knobbly-tyred cyclists.

The Tunnel End Inn was built around the same time as the canal and would have served ale to the leggers and thirsty boat crews who faced a claustrophobic struggle through the tunnel.

Inside the pub today there's still a roaring fire in winter and a cool drink in summer. It's a locals' pub with a welcoming 'join in' culture. Passing strangers are invited to tuck into a meat and tatty pie and a tipple before they set off on their way with a warm feeling and a promise to return.

The Tunnel End Inn is rightly proud to be a Freehouse. The food and ale definitely won't disappoint and it's a CAMRA pub to prove it.

STANDEDGE VISITOR CENTRE
Gateway to Standedge Tunnel
- the highest, longest and deepest canal tunnel in Britain
opened 25th May 2001
by Lily Turner, daughter of David Whitehead
the fastest legger through the tunnel in 1914

Make a day of it...

Standedge Tunnel & Visitor Centre

Standedge Tunnel is the highest, longest and deepest tunnel anywhere on Britain's inland waterways, and is one of the Seven Wonders of the Waterways.

The tunnel stretches for over three miles from Marsden on one side of the Pennines to Diggle on the other side, and there are three ways to explore it: over the top, in the Visitor Centre, or by venturing into its dark dank depths.

For the brave who want to travel inside the tunnel, the Visitor Centre operates 30-minute guided trips in a glass-roofed boat.

On the first Saturday of the month, more ardent thrill-seekers can pre-book a three-hour through boat trip and then, for fun, hike back over the moor.

Learn all about the history of the tunnel and the canal in the Visitor Centre. The Centre also has a programme of events through the season from art exhibitions to craft workshops and a Classic car show.

T:01484 844298 www.standedge.co.uk
Visitor Centre admission free.

Marsden Shuttle

The Shuttle boat is run by volunteers from the Huddersfield Narrow Canal Society, and operates as a Water Taxi for the 12-minute trip by canal between Marsden train station and Standedge Tunnel.
Sundays and Bank Hols April to October.
T:01457 871800
www.huddersfieldcanal.com

Mikron Theatre

The famous travelling theatre company are based in Marsden. Since the early 1970s, they've toured the canal networks by narrowboat during the summer. They perform their plays in canalside venues and beer gardens. They also do a road tour off season. As a registered charity, they're always happy for support! Why not join the 'Friends of Mikron'? Keep up to date with their latest news, and find out their diary of performances and venues on their website.
www.mikron.org.uk

Wildlife and nature

Red grouse, skylarks, deer, meadow pipits, foxes and curlews are just some of the wildlife and birds you might see. And there's a rich variety of plants, grasses and mosses that are willing to thrive on the peaty ground.

Go for an amble along the water
Walk down the hill in front of the
pub to reach the canal. Turn right
to reach the mouth of the tunnel
and the café, or turn left to go to
Standedge Visitor Centre.
Continue past the Centre and over
the footbridge for a short stroll
along the towpath to Marsden.

Come at Festival time
Marsden folk harbour old legends
and use them as a good excuse
to party whenever they can.
Throughout the seasons, Morris
Dancers jingle for joy, swilling beer
between leaps. The Tunnel End Inn
is usually at the heart of Marsden's
festivals, from the Celtic Imbolc
Festival in February to Cuckoo Day
in April and Marsden's Jazz Festival
in October.

Pub nitty-gritty

Tunnel End Inn
Waters Road
Marsden
West Yorkshire
HD7 6NF
T:01484 844636
www.tunnelendinn.com

Opening hours

Tue - Fri 1700 - 2300
Sat, Sun & Bank Hols 1200 - 2300 (Sun to 2230). They're also happy to open outside these hours by prior arrangement.

Food

Fri 1800 - 2000, Sat 1200 - 1500 & 1800 - 2000, Sun 1200 - 1600. Also Wed 1800 - 2100 (Meat and Tatty Pie night). Traditional home-cooked food from pies to steaks. Sunday roasts. Children's menu. Veggie options.

Drink

Freehouse.

Permanent ales: Black Sheep Best Bitter, Timothy Taylor's Landlord.

Guest ales: Regular. Many from local breweries such as Copper Dragon.

Other drinks: Bottled ciders.

Other essentials

Dogs are very welcome (by the resident dog too!)

Wheelchair access

Real fire

GONGOOZLING

The pub sits just uphill from the tunnel entrance. The views are over stunning moorland rather than the waterside. After a pint and a bite, wander down to the water and join in the drama of the tales of boaters as they emerge from the tunnel, and watch the faces of those about to enter.

TIP

Local bus, train and boat info kept behind the bar - just ask.

Stay over

If you can't drag yourself away, the pub even has a self-contained apartment for the night.

THE DAY IN A NUTSHELL

Standedge Tunnel - one of the 7 Wonders of the Waterways.

Location

OS Grid ref: SE040120

Canal: Huddersfield Narrow Canal,
overlooking Standedge Tunnel

OS Explorer Map: OL21

How to get there

By train
Marsden
National Rail Enquiries T:08457 484950

By bus
Traveline T:0871 2002233

By car
Standedge Visitor Centre car park, or roadside

By boat
The Marsden Shuttle
Water Taxi for the 12-min trip between
Marsden Station and Standedge Tunnel.
Sun/Bank Hols Apr - Oct.
T:01457 871800 www.huddersfieldcanal.com

Moorings
Moorings only for boats booked to go through
the tunnel.

Local Tourist info

Marsden Information Point
T:01484 845595 www.kirklees.gov.uk

'Welcome to Marsden' Exhibition
In the National Trust Estate Office by Marsden
railway station. Displays, leaflets and info
about Marsden and Upper Colne Valley.
Open daily 0900-1700.
T: 01484 847016 www.nationaltrust.org.uk

Huddersfield Narrow Canal Society
Set up in 1974, the Society campaigned
vigorously (and successfully) for the complete
restoration of the canal. They now concentrate
on its maintenance and promotion.
T:01457 871800 www.huddersfieldcanal.com

Fleur de Lys

A pub's reputation relies on its atmosphere and ale, and the Fleur de Lys can please you with both – yet it's most likely to be its pies you'll go home raving about, after a day out that has to include lunch at this pub.

For over 60 years, Midlanders have harboured a glint in their eye at the mention of the special home-baked Fleur de Lys pies made on these premises.

The success of the original recipe led to mass production that had to be outsourced onto an assembly line after the 1950s; but thankfully the pies are now baked here in the pub again with the indefinable touch of rolling-pin-love that factories can never quite manage.

There are eight different pies to tempt you with names such as Chicken of Aragon (free-range British chicken, smoky bacon, roast garlic, vermouth and fresh tarragon) or Matador (free-range British beef steak, chorizo, olives, tomato, sherry and butter beans).

And if you're a veggie, bored with the usual insult of mono-menus that add on a token cardboard-vegetarian lasagne, the Fleur de Lys invites you to roll up your sleeves and tuck into a flavour-bursting Heidi Pie (goat's cheese, sweet potato, spinach, red onion and roasted garlic).

The ancient structure of the pub building is as interesting as the pastry. A series of small rooms lead into each other where the former blacksmith's cottage now joins its neighbouring cottages to shape today's pub. History sits well in the leaded windows, exposed timber and low beams, yet a modern tint lightens the décor. This is a comfy old pub, with flagstoned floors, real fires and a civilised air.

And for added authenticity, there's a bar full of ghosts (even the sober say they've seen them, so it must be true).

Outside, there is a patio area close to the pub and a huge beer garden along the canalside. There are plenty of wooden tables and chairs on an expanse of grass at the water's edge, and on a summer's day, what could be better than sitting with your pint watching narrowboats pass by?

Watch out for the ducks though – they've heard about the pies and are willing to trample your dog to catch a falling crumb.

Make a day of it...

Sightseeing

Coming to the Fleur de Lys is the perfect excuse to leave the mania of Stratford sightseeing behind. Escape the rush of trying to cram in all the Shakespearian tourist attractions. We think if Shakespeare was still around, he'd be tucking into a pie at the Fleur de Lys!

The Stratford-upon-Avon Canal has its own sightseeing delights to explore. To get to the towpath (on the opposite side of the water), turn left out of the pub. The lane heads to the canal.

Split bridges

Many of the traditional lock bridges along the Stratford Canal were built in two sections, with a gap down the centre. When working boats were being towed by horses, the gap allowed the rope to slip through, rather than having to untie the horse from the boat. This saved crucial time (and money) for the working boat crews. Split bridges are scattered along this canal, with the nearest one to the pub just a short stroll along the towpath, next to lock 34.

Aqueducts

The Stratford-upon-Avon Canal has three unusual aqueducts. Uniquely, the towpath is lower than the water level. This gives the novel experience of being able to walk alongside a cast-iron trough full of water not unlike a bathtub! And if a narrowboat happens to pass by, it's even more exciting.

Yarningale Aqueduct, the smallest of the three, is just a short stroll along the towpath from the pub, next to lock 34.

Barrel-roofed cottages

A quirky feature of this canal is its mysteriously barrel-roofed lock cottages that line the water. There's a purely practical truth behind the quirk - engineers building the Stratford Canal knew more about building curved bridges than houses so when they came to build lock cottages for the lengthsmen, they adapted their skills. The result was cottages with curious barrel-shaped roofs. One of these cottages is next to lock 31, across the canal from the Fleur de Lys. 'Lengthsman's Cottage' is available for holiday lets.
T:01628 825925
www.landmarktrust.org.uk

Pub nitty-gritty

Fleur de Lys
Lapworth Street
Lowsonford
Henley-in-Arden
Warwickshire
B95 5HJ
T:01564 782431
www.fleurdelys-lowsonford.com

Opening hours

Mon - Sat 1100 - 2300.
Sun 1200 - 2230.

Food

Mon - Fri 1200 - 2100, Sat 1200 - 2130, Sun 1200 - 2000. Renowned for their great pies. Wide choice of other food. Child options on the menu. Veggie options.

Drink

Family-owned business.

Permanent ales: Greene King IPA & Abbot.

Guest ales: Changed weekly.

Member of Greene King Head Brewer's Club in recognition of keeping excellent cask ales.

Other drinks: Speciality Coffees. Choice of lagers including Leffe, and cider.

Other essentials

Dog-friendly. The pub supports the Kennel Club's 'Open for Dogs' campaign. www.openfordogs.org.uk

Wheelchair access (assistance on hand for steps in lower part of pub)

Real fires (six!)

The pub has an indoor skittle alley available for groups to use free of charge (subject to prior notice).

GONGOOZLING

It's right by the lock, and boats are constantly moored directly opposite.

TIP

Once you've tasted one of the pub's pies, you'll want to try the rest. Join the Fleur de Lys Pie Club. Membership entitles you to 20% off your main meal whenever you visit.

(Stratford-upon-Avon Canal Society) SONACS

Like most canals the Stratford has at times faced struggles for its survival. In 1959 passionate protests riled against the canal's closure and gutsy restoration work from volunteers led to this stretch of the canal being reopened in 1964. Scattered along the canal you'll spot plaques commemorating its reopening that read, "we were not experts therefore we did not know what could not be done".

THE DAY IN A NUTSHELL

Pies and passing boats.

Location

OS Grid ref: SP187679

Canal: Stratford-upon-Avon Canal, by lock 31

OS Explorer Map: 220

How to get there

By train
Nearest station is Lapworth
National Rail Enquiries T:08457 484950

By bus
Traveline T:0871 2002233

By car
Pub car park

By boat
Anglo Welsh Waterways Holidays have day boat hire from Wootton Wawen.
T:0117 3041122 www.anglowelsh.co.uk

Moorings
Plenty of moorings opposite the pub, above and below the lock. Pub patrons can also moor alongside the pub's beer garden.

Local Tourist info

Stratford-upon-Avon Tourist Information Centre
T:0870 1607930
www.shakespeare-country.co.uk

Stratford-upon-Avon Canal Society (Sonacs)
Formed in 1956, the society's objectives include the use, maintenance and improvement of all inland waterways, especially the Stratford-upon-Avon Canal.
T:01564 783672
www.stratfordcanalsociety.org.uk

Shakespeare Birthplace Trust
Stratford-upon-Avon. T:01789 296083
www.shakespeare.org.uk

Clock Warehouse
Trent & Mersey Canal

The Clock Warehouse pub is a stunning chameleon, sitting just off the A6 in an East Midlands landscape. Carloads of empty tummies turn up at this foodie pub. Children are explicitly welcome, and their great grannies too. Yet behind the fizzy drinks and fuss, there's a fascinating adventure for the discerning eye.

This is a day out all about buildings. Shardlow is a satisfying example of an inland port and the ancient buildings that once served the canalside community. There have been people living in the area since the Doomsday Book, but it was when the Trent & Mersey Canal arrived that warehouses sprung up and the population of the village thrived.

The canal was built by the clout of Josiah Wedgwood's pottery business and the engineering skills of James Brindley, but inevitably when commerce abandoned the waterways, many of the canalside buildings were threatened. Luckily, in the late 1970s, much of the canalside became a designated conservation area and a walk along the towpath reveals old warehouses now turned into private use.

It's easy to imagine the important landowners who might once have lived inside the grandest houses. And, as you'd expect, there are a lot of pubs along the canal that would have kept beer for the ordinary workers. The Malt Shovel, built in 1799, once had a brewery attached and stored barrels of ale along the canal (typical of many traditional canalside pubs).

Some buildings predate the canal, such as the tiny white teashop just across the water from the pub, but most buildings tell a story of either the canal past or present. The biggest building by far, and definitely the most commanding, is the 18th-century Trent Mill, which is now the Clock Warehouse pub. It has instant appeal on the outside, and inside it has creaky floorboards and history struggling to contain itself behind the mountains of chips and jolly music.

Don't arrive expecting the homely landlady with a robust tongue and a warm hug that you get in some canalside pubs: here you're met by staff wearing uniform T-shirts and busy smiles. The pub is on several levels, with a collection of rooms. The bar on the main floor is decorated with canal pictures and traditional canal art which does its best to mask the game machine tucked in the corner.

Downstairs you can play darts and pool and have a view over the water at the same time. This room leads into the arch inside the old warehouse where narrowboats would have once loaded and unloaded cargo. Through the glass panels, you can see a narrowboat display.

The whole pub is a fascinating exhibition of contrived canalia, but the authenticity of its history floats straight through its brickwork and great wooden beams.

There's never a dull moment inside, but when the sun shines everyone wants to be outside. And there are huge grassy spaces to sprawl out along the waterside and gongoozle until the heart is content.

Make a day of it...

Visit Shardlow, the canal village

From the pub, cross the canal at the lock and you can saunter either way along the canal towpath.

But if you turn left and follow the canal, it will take you all the way to the very start of the Trent & Mersey Canal where it meets the River Trent. Derwent Mouth Lock ingeniously tames a branch of water from the river allowing the canal to begin on its way.

Standing at the start of this 93-mile canal is, bizarrely, absolutely thrilling. On the one hand, it's just the idea of personally adventuring to a landmark, and on the other it's a finger pointing out the beautiful arrogance of those Victorian entrepreneurs and engineers who cut water-roads wherever they would, and defied anything to get in their way.

Pubs and old warehouses line the route and, in summer there are boats to watch. You'll probably see more cruisers and river boats than is normal on a narrow canal because of this canal's proximity to the river.

The towpath is rugged and not over-kempt. Ignore the pong of sewage around Derwent Mouth Lock, it's short-lived and it's easy to cheer up when you see swans, shags, all sorts of wildlife and the glorious conker tree by the lock.

The gentle amble in an undisturbed flat landscape is briefly invaded by road noise from the distance: there's irony in the distraction, when today's peaceful canal was once the bustling commercial transport route itself.

Cargoes which came on wide boats from the river were stored in the canalside warehouses before being reloaded onto narrowboats to be transported along the canal. There are over 50 listed buildings in Shardlow, and the sense of history is tangible.

Shardlow Heritage Centre has a Village Trail leaflet for sale, which takes you through the buildings one by one, explaining what their original purpose used to be. The volunteers who run the centre are also happy to organise special guided tours for groups.

Mileposts

Canal mileposts normally measure the miles from the start of a canal to the end. The cast-iron mileposts on the Trent & Mersey Canal unusually start counting from Shardlow rather than from the start of the canal by the first lock at Derwent Mouth.

The mileposts were removed during World War II but the Trent & Mersey Canal Society spent several years in the late '70s restoring and replacing all 92 mileposts along the canal. All original mileposts are now Grade II-listed.

Shardlow Heritage centre

The Salt Warehouse is the oldest canal warehouse in the village and, fittingly, now houses Shardlow Heritage Centre. For a very small entrance fee, you can learn about the fascinating history of this area. Among its exhibits is a replica of a working boat family's cabin.

It's the sort of heritage centre that is a labour of love and manned with passion, so anything you can think of to ask is enthusiastically answered!

Open Easter - Oct. Sat, Sun & Bank Hols 1200 - 1700 (accompanied children free admittance). Wheelchair access. T:01332 793368

Pub nitty-gritty

Clock Warehouse
London Road
Shardlow
Derby
Derbyshire
DE72 2HL
T:01332 792844
www.clockwarehousepub.co.uk

Opening hours

Mon - Sat 1100 - 2300.
Sun 1200 - 2230.

Food

Daily 1200 - 2100. Menu has the usual combos, Cajun chicken and 2 for £10, and interesting-sounding extras such as the Crockpot or special 'Fish on Friday'. Good family 'X' factor. Children's menu (children eat free on Saturdays). Veggie options.

Drink

Marston's pub.

Permanent ales: Marston's Pedigree & Marston's Smooth.

Guest ales: Regular. Includes Marston's beers and others such as Wychwood's Hobgoblin.

Other drinks: Wine menu.

Other essentials

Wheelchair access

No dogs allowed inside the pub

GONGOOZLING

There's a grassy space with tables under weeping willows just outside the pub, which gives a great water-level viewpoint of boats entering or leaving the lock.

TIP

Don't miss out on a visit to the loos.

They are possibly the most canalia-decorated we've seen (we could only go in the girls, so can't vouch for the boys!)

THE DAY IN A NUTSHELL

A journey into the trade heritage of one of Britain's first canals.

Location

OS Grid ref: SK440302

Canal: Trent & Mersey Canal, next to Shardlow Lock

OS Explorer Map: 245

How to get there

By train
Nearest station is Derby
National Rail Enquiries T:08457 484950

By bus
Traveline T:0871 2002233

By car
Large pub car park

By boat
Hire a Canalboat Ltd
Short break and holiday boat hire from Sawley Marina on the River Trent.
T:0800 3893022 www.hireacanalboat.co.uk

Moorings
The village has a large marina near Derwent Mouth Lock. The best moorings would be either along the stretch leading to the lock, or above Shardlow Lock near the pub.

Local Tourist info

Shardlow Heritage Centre
Canalside by the Clock Warehouse.
T:01332 793368

Derbyshire Tourist info
www.derbyshireuk.net
www.visitderbyshire.co.uk

Tap & Spile
Birmingham Canal Navigations

The Bullring, the markets, Symphony Hall, Anthony Gormley's sculpture, designer shopping at the Mailbox, multi-cultural panache and lots of people who speak like Julie Walters. That's Birmingham.

But first impressions don't give away the city's biggest secret. It's the capital of Britain's canals with more miles of waterway than Venice. Without a gondola in sight, Birmingham's water is less extrovertly romantic than Venice's, but never underestimate Brummie passions.

Where the modern architecture of the skyline meets the canal basin, a powerful aesthetic is the pride of Birmingham. The canal hub isn't a grimy leftover from the past, it's a lovingly regenerated meeting place between the old and the new. The canal isn't exactly hiding from the city, it just waits quietly below the bridge, reached by steps leading down from the urban flurry into its parallel waterworld. A slow haven a few yards, and a million more, from the unwholesome anxiety of city-consumerism blindly frogmarching past.

The famous water area known as Brindley Place leads from Gas Street Basin. Brindley, the indomitable engineer responsible for much of Britain's original canal building, would probably approve of this millenium's waterway through Birmingham. Its purpose has changed, but its architectural integrity remains.

Disrespecting the architecture, a gargoyle of clubland straddles Broad Street above the bridge over the canal, but there's a wide choice of pubs and cafés along the canal for a more discerning light lunch.

For good, and even great, beer go straight to the Tap and Spile. It's the sort of pub where if you ask for your pint of ale to be pulled without a sprinkler, you won't get a blank look or a tut. From the minute you arrive, the welcome is real. An elusive canalside door set unceremoniously into unspoilt brickwork lures the pub-goer from the cut.

Inside, a hunky wooden bar rubs up to red brick walls and the bare sounds of old floorboards announce your arrival. A distinguished display of taps paints the beery culture, but there are impressive continental lagers behind the bar and it's just as easy to come and have a Jagermeister or a Smirnoff and lime.

The Tap and Spile was a warehouse in a former life, and now it's a casually intimate pub that's utterly non-pretentious. Very likeable. And a must for Old Peculiar fans!

2

WORCESTER BAR (1792)

This bar separates the Birmingham from the Worcester and Birmingham canals. All cargo was manhandled across until the Bar lock was added in 1815.

Make a day of it...

Along the canal

The water's past harps on about smells of smoke and coal dust, sounds of boats loading and unloading cargoes of porcelain and glass, and winds that wafted chocolate crumb destined for the Cadbury's factory. Today it's rightfully alive again with meandering trip boats crammed with wide-eyed passengers.

The National Indoor Arena, the National Sealife Centre, trendy bars and cafés line the water, yet heritage hides in every nook and cranny. Look under the bridges and gouged ropemarks are visible where horses once tugged boats. Peer into unspoilt waterside buildings.

Admire the cast-iron bridges. But don't tell the tourists one of the bridges is a recently-made fake. Made from the Horseley design, in 1988, at a cost of £18,000, it was the first cast-iron bridge to be made in over 100 years (not cheating, just new history making).

Gas Street Basin

Historically, the importance of the basin has a clue in its name: Gas Street Basin was the first zone in the city to have newfangled gas lights. It was the busy point where the Worcester & Birmingham Canal met the Birmingham Canal Navigations (BCN) Main Line.

Canal companies were precious about their water and competition was fierce in the canalmania years of the Industrial Revolution.

In a bid not to lose their water, the BCN insisted a solid bar was built to separate its canal from the Worcester & Birmingham Canal. The Worcester Bar was built in 1792 and remained for 30 Berlinesque years, forcing cargoes to be laboriously lifted over the bar.

The major inconvenience saw sense in 1815 and a cut was made through the bar and a lock built to allow boats through. The lock has now gone but the bar still exists with its cut through allowing narrowboats today the freedom to roam.

Catch the waterbus

Queue up at the bus stop to catch the waterbus in the heart of Birmingham's canals. Jump on near the pub in Gas Street Basin, and make your first stop the Mailbox for some glamorous shopping. Then hop back on the bus to explore Brindley Place.

T:0121 4556163
www.sherbornewharf.co.uk

Food afloat

Make lunch even more special by eating afloat on a narrowboat. There's coffee and light bites on the George at Brindley Place, or stay till dark and go on a 3-hour dinner cruise with Away2dine from the Mailbox (Sunday Roast Cruises too)

The Floating Coffee Company
T:0121 6330050 www.sherbornewharf.co.uk

Away2dine
T:0845 6445244 www.away2dine.co.uk

Canalside Café

On the canal side overlooking Gas Street Basin. Once the lock keeper's cottage, it's now a rustic, garlicky place that's a quirky pub-café-restaurant all rolled into one. A relaxed city hang-out for a waterside drink. Veggie haven.

Canalside Café
T:0121 2487979

Pub nitty-gritty

The Tap & Spile
Gas Street
Birmingham
West Midlands
B1 2JT
T:0121 6325602
www.tapandspilebirmingham.co.uk

Opening hours

Daily 1200 - 0400. (Entertainment Thu - Sat 2200 - 0400).

Food

Bar snacks only on weekend evenings.

Drink

Freehouse

Permanent ales: Greene King Old Speckled Hen, Greene King IPA, Young's Bitter, Fuller's London Pride.

Guest ales: Regular. Huge range including Theakston's Old Peculier.

Other drinks: Good choice of Continental and American lagers and bottled beers.

Other essentials

No dogs allowed in the pub

Wheelchair access

GONGOOZLING

No grassy beer garden but the pub overlooks the water.

TIP

Anyone of a quiet disposition should leave before dusk, especially at weekends. It's a bit too close to Broad Street's clubland and can get rammed full.

THE DAY IN A NUTSHELL

Great ale in the canal capital.

Location

OS Grid ref: SP062865

Canal: Birmingham Canal Navigations, in Gas Street Basin

OS Explorer Map: 220

How to get there

By train
Birmingham New Street, Moor Street & Snow Hill
National Rail Enquiries T:08457 484950

By bus
Traveline T:0871 2002233

By car
Roadside or various city centre car parks

By boat
City Heritage Cruises from the International Convention Centre, Brindley Place.
Easter to October 4 times daily (weekends only in winter)
T:0121 4556163
www.sherbornewharf.co.uk

Moorings
There are convenient visitor moorings near the Mailbox and Brindley Place.

Local Tourist info

Birmingham Tourism Centre
T:0844 8883883

Birmingham website
www.visitbirmingham.com

The Star Inn
Monmouthshire & Brecon Canal

Another sociable waterside pub for a simple day out, grazing on hearty canal traditions of conversation and community. The Star flings its doors open to local canal folk and landlubbers alike, as well as passing strangers travelling through by boat, bike or boot (or car if you have to).

It's a mixture of folk that gel easily in the laid-back ambience of this corner of Wales. On cold days, huddle in the bar, sharing long communal tables with a huge log fire centrepiece. Have a game of pool or while away any wet afternoon with ready supplies of board games curling at their edges for anyone's use.

The ale is fit for discerning beer bellies and the food is plain and good. Their Ploughman's comes with tasty Welsh cheddar to remind you where you are.

When the sun is out, it's a treat to sit in the spacious garden. Although the Star Inn is canalside, the canal is at a higher level than the garden, so you can't actually see the water. Welsh stone walling unfortunately hides the water from view, but makes the garden a chilled retreat from boating activity.

Just above the beer garden, the canal is carried over the river by an aqueduct. Inside the pub, you're never in any doubt about the proximity of the pub to the canal when you look at the set of photos on the wall. They show the pub up to its knees in canal water following a catastrophic breach of the aqueduct in 1994.

The river tumbles beyond the bottom of the garden doing its best to sooth with sloshing sounds of tranquillity and the occasional bird joining in.

Welsh Spaniels mingle with Labradors and Westies, and dogs that can leap the low boundary wall get a river paddle for free. It's a spoonful of water therapy with the hubbub of chatter, but drag yourself away to explore the canal if you can.

Make a day of it...

Limekilns and quarries

The Brecon Beacons are synonymous with the outdoors. It's got hills and healthy adventures yet, behind the scenes, the canal keeps the secret of a different past.

Towards the edge of the village of Talybont-on-Usk, there's a reminder of the area's industrial heritage. A display board and model tram tell the story of how limestone and coal was quarried up in the hills above Talybont, then brought down to the canal on an 8-mile long tramroad.

Once it arrived at Talybont, the rock was put into the burning hot limekilns (the remains of the kilns are on the opposite side of the canal) to be broken down into quicklime. This was then transferred to barrels to be loaded onto waiting narrowboats.

You can follow the path of the original tramroad from just above bridge 143, by the White Hart pub, up into the hills.

A walking guide to the tramroad route is available in the pub.

Hire a day boat

You can always hire a holiday narrowboat from one of the Mon & Brec's hireboat operators. But, if you fancy hiring a boat for just an hour or a day, Brecon Boats have small 5-seater day boats for hire from the Traveller's Rest pub.

Booking ahead is advisable during the busy summer season.
T:01874 676401

The Taff Trail Cycle Route

The Trail follows the Mon & Brec Canal from just outside Brecon to Brynich Lock where cyclists head off to continue along the road. Because of the narrowness of the canal towpath in this area, cycling is not allowed on the next stretch, but walkers on the Trail can continue along the canal to Talybont-on-Usk.

Pub crawl

Talybont is blessed with a number of pubs so you could just do a mini pub crawl along the canal towpath. From the Star to the White Hart, to the Traveller's Rest, and then into the village to the Usk Inn.

Pub nitty-gritty

The Star Inn
Talybont-on-Usk
Brecon
Powys
LD3 7YX
T:01874 676635
www.starinntalybont.co.uk

Opening hours

Mon - Fri 1130 - 1500 & 1700 - 2330.
All day Sat, Sun and summer.

Food

Daily 1200 - 1430 & 1800 - 2100. They try
to source local products where possible for
home-made traditional pub meals. Veggie
options.

Drink

Freehouse

Constantly changing ales, over 500 each
year from all over the UK (from Cornwall to
Scotland!). Ales from as many local breweries
as possible, including Breconshire Brewery.

Other essentials

Dogs are welcome as long as they are
well-behaved and on a lead (including in the
garden).

Wheelchair access

Real fire

The Star also does B&B if you want to stay a
bit longer.

Live music last Friday of every month

Brecknock CAMRA Pub of the Year 2009

GONGOOZLING

You may not be able to
gongoozle boats from
the garden but the lush
greenery surrounding the
pub more than makes up
for it.

TIP

In summer, the Mon &
Brec Canal is busy with
boats, walkers and cyclists.
Outside of the holiday
season, it's a quieter
story, and if you come in
autumn, this tree-lined
canal puts on a spectacular
show.

THE DAY IN A NUTSHELL

Beer by the water in the
Breacon Beacons National
Park.

Location

OS Grid ref: **SO114226**

Canal: **Monmouthshire & Brecon Canal, by the aqueduct**

OS Explorer Map: **OL13/OL12**

How to get there

By train
Nearest station is Abergavenny
National Rail Enquiries T:08457 484950

By bus
Traveline Cymru T:0871 2002233

Beacons Bus
A great way to combine walking on the canal and the Beacons. Walk one way then get the bus back. T:01873 853254

By car
Roadside near the canal

By boat
Brecon Boats
Talybont. Day boat hire. T:01874 676401

Moorings
There's a water point on the towpath just above the pub, and convenient moorings throughout the village.

Local Tourist info

Tourist Information Centre
Brecon. T:01874 622485
www.breconbeaconstourism.co.uk

Brecon Beacons National Park
T:01874 624437
www.breconbeacons.org

Monmouthshire, Brecon & Abergavenny
Canals Trust
Established in 1984, the Trust aims to promote and restore the entire length of the canal.
T:01633 892167
www.mon-brec-canal-trust.org.uk

Foxton Locks Inn
Grand Union Canal

Gnarled villages, undulating bridleways and lush scarecrow countryside lead to Foxton Locks. If you're arriving by car, even the leafy car park is inviting, but don't just pull out your picnic and stay next to your car all day - this is only the start of a fascinating waterways trail.

British Waterways (BW) have created a trail marked by arrows tiled into the ground and posts. Follow the route through the trees and you arrive at the canal, where you can choose to turn left to get to Leicester and right to reach London... or just keep following the arrows for a much lazier pub day out. Foxton Locks may be practically in the middle of nowhere, but it isn't a forgotten overgrown canal zone – it expects visitors, and gets them.

The lock flight and the canal surroundings have been sensitively sculpted to keep history living. When you first reach Top Lock, soaring views of green England force you to stop and inhale. Then the teashop tempts you with creature comforts: cream teas, farmhouse ice cream and you can even buy a souvenir mug to take home. As well as your cuppa you get to meet John Cryer, a life-sized model of the former lock-keeper during the canal's heyday. Stand next to John and gaze with him out of the window overlooking the lock. Even sceptics of over-contrived canal antiquities (yes, that's us) can't help but melt as a be-capped John grips his mug of stone cold, solid tea and witters in a pre-recorded voice about his locks.

The old stables next door have been turned into a discovery room with displays and info about the 50-60 horses and boats that originally travelled through the locks every day. Today boaters have to book in with the lock-keeper and pass by in gluts. The staircase flight has 10 locks, climbing 75 feet and using 25,000 gallons of water with every boat that travels through. It's a challenge for boat crews and bound to raise emotions one way or another! If you wanted, you could gongoozle here all day and never get bored: but the pub always lurks patiently at the bottom of the flight.

On the other side of the water from the Foxton Locks Inn is the unusual Bridge 61 pub. Call in for a 4-pint pitcher of ale, a pint of milk or even a loaf of bread and some pickled eggs. This quirky shop-pub defies the rules. Bridge 61 is an unusual mini-pub that gives the impression it's part of the cogs of the area, quietly getting on with its own business while the Foxton Locks Inn provides everything else visitors could want.

First impressions inside the Foxton Locks Inn didn't immediately win our affections since we prefer a pub to feel pubby first and foodie second. At busy times it welcomes eaters with friendly centurions to take you to your table. But the food is good, the ambience is happy, and after sitting outside on the water's edge with a pint of scrumptious Theakston Grouse Beater, we were irretrievably hooked.

The pub's beer garden is right by the junction to the lock flight, overlooking queues of boats and their manoeuvring antics. Gongoozling is the only distraction from the pub's well-kept real ale and delicious food.

This is a pub really in the hub of the canal zone at Foxton Locks making it the perfect day out with everything right on the spot.

Make a day of it...

Foxton Inclined Plane & Canal Museum

After you've wallowed in as much food and drink as you want, go for a wander around the waterside.

Climb the hill to the purpose-built balcony overlooking the remains of the inclined plane. It's an acropolis of canal heritage with the rubble of carriage tracks tantilizingly almost intact. The plane was designed to lift boats up Foxton hill in a fraction of the time taken to work through the 10 locks of the staircase flight.

On the 10th July 1900, crowds dressed up in Panama hats and excitement to celebrate its opening. Sadly it closed in 1911 but ambitious plans are afoot for its restoration. The Panama hats may have gone, but if the Foxton Inclined Plane Trust get their way, there"ll be celebrations again at its reopening.

The Trust's headquarters (in the old lift's boiler house), now also houses a small museum.

Summer open daily 1000-1700. Weekends 1000-1600 Nov-Mar (ring re weekdays). T:01162 792657 www.fipt.org.uk

Foxton Locks

The whole place behaves like an outdoor museum, alive and kicking, with boats still ploughing through the locks in exactly the same way as they would have over 200 years ago.

Narrowboats these days can be luxury floating cottages with all mod-cons onboard, yet working narrowboats of the past carried cargoes of sugar, tea, soap, tinned food, chemicals and paper.

The scene at Foxton is virtually unchanged except the lock-keepers cottages and old stables have become pubs, shops and tearooms. www.foxtonlocks.com

Go on a boat trip

'Vagabond' is a vintage boat, reputed to be over 100 years old, with a fixed roof to protect you from the weather and open sides for the views. 25-minute cruise.

Sundays, Bank Hols, some Saturdays & school holiday weekday afternoons (weather permitting).

Hire a boat for the day

Foxton Boats has day boats that can be hired for half or full days.

Boats are for up to 12 people (and you can take your dog too). T:01162 792285 www.foxtonboats.co.uk

Pub nitty-gritty

Foxton Locks Inn
Bottom Lock
Gumley Road
Foxton
Leicestershire
LE16 7RA
T:01162 791515
www.restaurantfoxtonlocks.co.uk

Opening hours

All day every day 1100 - 2300 (winter hours
vary - they tend to close earlier in the evening).

Food

Main menu 1200 - 1500 & 1800 - 2045,
Sundays 1200 - 1545 & 1800 - 1930. Snacks
served 1100 - 1800 every day. Good selection
of food for any time of day, from morning
cakes to tapas. Child menu. Veggie options.

Drink

Waterside Pubs Partnership between British
Waterways and Scottish & Newcastle.

Permanent ales: Theakston's Old Peculier &
Black Bull, Greene King Old Speckled Hen,
Caeldonian Deuchars IPA.

Guest ales: Range of weekly changing guest
and seasonal ales, such as Theakston's
Grouse Beater.

Other drinks:
Extensive 110-bin selection of wines.

Cask Marque Accreditation

Other essentials

Dogs are welcome outdoors and you can book
a table inside to take your dog in with you.

Wheelchair access

New canalside function room available for
private hire

GONGOOZLING

Great for gongoozling as
it's right on the junction
by the locks. Fantastic
views over the canal and
countryside.

TIP

Don't leave the Foxton
Locks Inn without going
to the loo. As in many
canal pubs, the corridor
to the toilets doubles up
as a mini art gallery of
colourful canal pictures
and artefacts.

THE DAY IN A NUTSHELL

Not just a day out - it's
a designated trail of
discovery, and the Foxton
Locks is a must for real
ale fans.

Location

OS Grid ref: **SP691897**

Canal: **Grand Union Canal (Leicester Section),**
at the foot of Foxton Locks

OS Explorer Map: **233**

How to get there

By train
Nearest station is Market Harborough
National Rail Enquiries T:08457 484950

By bus
Traveline T:0871 2002233

By car
BW car park (charge), short walk from canal

By boat
During the summer, boats are guided through
the Foxton Locks Flight by the lock-keepers
(there daily from 0800 - 1900).

Foxton Boats
Day boat hire and a trip boat - trips from
Foxton Bottom Lock Sun, Bank Hols, some
Sat and weekday afternoons during school
holidays (dep weather).
T:01162 792285 www.foxtonboats.co.uk

Moorings
No mooring right outside the pub, but plenty of
mooring along the stretch beyond the bridge.

Local Tourist info

Market Harborough Tourist Information
T:01858 821270
www.goleicestershire.com

Foxton Locks website
www.foxtonlocks.com

Shroppie Fly
Shropshire Union Canal

You could imagine yourself sitting here in your slippers on a winter's night in front of the open fire. We arrived in shoes on a Wednesday lunchtime in summer.

The Shroppie Fly whistles with ordinariness as it goes about its business. Inside it could be just like any other not-posh pub, except that it's got a real narrowboat as a bar. Understandably, you won't notice the unspectacular tables, chairs, carpet or the click click of the pool table in the background. But even though it's hard to pull your eyes from the retired narrowboat that's adorned incongruously with optics and beer taps, you should catch hard-backed wafts of booky charm from rows of full bookshelves throughout the bar.

This pub plays riddles from the minute you arrive. We thought we'd made a wrong turn off the Shroppie Canal and landed on Le Canal du Midi somewhere in rural France. Huge hanging baskets of red geraniums greeted us, bouncing sunshine onto the cream-coloured pub frontage, with dashes of blue paint dancing around the windows. A rustic boater lazing on an even more rustic bench by the pub's door added to our delusion, until he nodded "hello" not "bonjour".

The seating outside faces the canal and feels less intimate than inside, with waterway travellers passing by all day. Dogs are welcomed with water bowls, and tables line the water's edge so close you could dangle your feet in if the fancy took. The Shropshire Union is popular with holiday boaters and locals tell us that, in summer, more than 30 boats a day can cruise by.

Everything is about boats here, even the pub's name. A Shroppie Fly was a type of narrowboat designed for speed in the early days of the canals; and these boats that once 'flew' along the Shropshire Union Canal were prestigious. As they still are now, of course.

In a former life, the pub was a cheese warehouse and luckily the 'speedy' narrowboats of the Shropshire Union would have helped to keep the good reputation of Cheshire Cheese as it was transported, still fresh, to its destinations.

Allow extra time to go to the loo – not because the loos are anything to talk about – but because the corridor leading to both the ladies and gents is a mirage of old photographs, ropes, fascinating maps and stories of the famous boats behind the pub's name.

Canal pubs love to talk about boats, and nobody is going to yawn at that, but hiding behind all the boaty stuff you get a sense that music is a big thing here too. If you miss the live music and evenings of karaoke, you'll probably hear a radio humming quietly in the background during the day as it would from your own kitchen. The casual air of this place just happens.

If you're eating here, come with a willing belly. The portions are generous and you'll have to open your jaws wide to fit the brick-sized chips in.

The Shroppie Fly is an everyday pub with extraordinary enchantment.

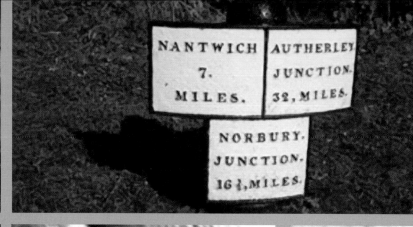

NANTWICH 7. MILES.

AUTHERLEY JUNCTION. 32, MILES.

NORBURY. JUNCTION. 16¾, MILES.

Make a day of it...

Visit Audlem, the canal village

You're as likely to see a tractor rolling down the main street as a car. The village is small and community life is clearly valued. Award plaques are everywhere: 'Best kept village', 'Village of the year' 'Community Pride'.

The commemorative statue in the centre isn't about the trials of war; it celebrates a surgeon of the 1800s who spent his life saving others.

The church sits in the heart of the village. Its 13th-century door is a stunner, and even more stunning is that it wasn't locked when we passed through this refreshingly trusting village.

A community tapestry made by men, women and children of lovely Audlem hangs inside the church. Embroidered words speak volumes 'to hafe forbearance if things do not sometimes go on quite right'.

You get the feeling it's the sort of place songs should be written about; somewhere the WI could go naked and be applauded because they're local.

Tourism isn't glossy here, Audlem is a place plenty pass through. There's a steady drift of cyclists, walkers, boaters, travellers from the Weaver Way and the canal.

Audlem Mill (canalside by the pub)

Enter the Mill and it'll be some time before you're willing to leave. Not only is there an impressive collection of canal books to look at but also craft kits, art, wool, needle craft, cross stitch, postcards and all canalia. Craft & needlework courses in winter. Art exhibition at Easter. And if you hear paws tapping on a keyboard behind the counter, don't be alarmed: it'll just be Winston, Audlem Mill's 'dog with a blog'. An unassuming cocker spaniel with even more superior communication skills online than in the flesh.

T:01270 811059
www.audlemmill.co.uk

Keep your eyes peeled for

In 2000, the villagers buried a 'Millenium Time capsule' containing aspects of village life at the turn of the century. A metre-long tube is buried underneath a quartz millstone. Its plaque ends with the sentiment of this village: 'By the Village - for the Village'.

Go for an amble along the water

If you can drag yourself away from the pub, go for an amble along the towpath into a canal landscape with country smells. Turn left out of the pub to go up Audlem Lock Flight. The views of the countryside are unblemished, uncluttered and utterly Cheshire.

A peaceful stroll with water, big skies, ochre and green fields dotted with oaks and dragonflies... and more than a strong hint of the transport route it once was.

Keep your eyes peeled for

The (heart-warming) trust of a local farmer who displays produce on the canalside with a 'help yourself' note and honesty box for money.

Hidden heritage

Look out for the rope marks and gouges on the undersides of the bridges where boat horses once heaved and tugged working boats laden with cargo.

Pub nitty-gritty

Shroppie Fly
The Wharf
Shropshire Street
Audlem
Cheshire
CW3 0DX
T: 01270 811772
www.shroppiefly.co.uk

Opening hours
All day (1100 - 2300 summer, 1200 - 2300 winter).

Food
Daily 1200 - 2100 (2000 Sundays) in summer, lunchtimes & evenings in winter. Good home-cooked traditional pub food. Children's menu. Veggie options.

Drink
Punch Pub Group.

Permanent ales:
Timothy Taylor's Landlord, Courage Best.

Guest ales: Include Titanic Anchor and Courage Director's.

Other drinks: Good range of bottled beers & ciders.

Other essentials

Dog-friendly

Wheelchair access (no separate loo)

Real fires

Occasional Beer Festivals

Live music most Monday, Tuesday, Friday and Bank Holiday evenings. Mondays are folk jamming sessions with an open house culture.

GONGOOZLING
As the pub is between two locks, there are plenty of opportunities for gongoozling without even leaving your seat! On a good summer's day, grab a table outside for a vantage point right by the water..

TIP
Arrive at the pub, pull up a chair and snuggle up with your pint and a good read from one of the books on the shelves lining the pub walls.

THE DAY IN A NUTSHELL
Quirky bar and community spirit.

Location

OS Grid ref: **SJ657437**

Canal: **Shropshire Union Canal, by lock 13**

OS Explorer Map: **257**

How to get there

By train

Nearest stations are Nantwich & Whitchurch
(both approx 7 miles away)
National Rail Enquiries T:08457 484950

By bus

Traveline T:0871 2002233

By car

Large pub car park and free public car park off
Cheshire Street.

By boat

Welsh Gateway Canal Holidays
Nantwich. Holiday & day boat hire.
T:01270 624075
www.welshgatewaycanalholidays.co.uk
Nantwich Canal Centre
Nantwich. Day boat hire.
T:01270 625122
www.nantwichcanalcentre.co.uk

Moorings

There's a water point just outside the pub, and
convenient 48-hour visitor moorings above
lock 12. But If you want to escape the crowds
to watch the sunset go down, try the 48-hour
moorings between locks 2 and 3.

Local Tourist info

Tourist info point

Inside newsagents, Williams of Audlem
Open all day, every day. T:01270 811210

Audlem town website

www.audlem.org

Shropshire Union Canal society

www.shropshireunion.org.uk

The Turf
Exeter Ship Canal

A location to live for! Sandwiched on a petering edge of land blustering between the choppy estuary mouth on one side, and the spot where water is first tamed into the Exeter Ship Canal on the other, the Turf is a wild canalside pub, wrestling with nature's own elements and no less than a British treasure.

There's nothing feeble about the Turf, and even getting there is part of the thrill. Don't bother scratching at road maps to try and drive here by car – you can't. The only way is by boat, bike or boot, so just follow the water road and let yourself enjoy the special allegiance a car-free zone brings.

Arriving at this pub is an event and even if you just swill a quick lime and soda before heading off, you'll have had a grand day out. Whether you paddle, pedal or pace here, the water milks every moment that it can. Sounds of boats carry along the canal water, but you don't hear the usual putt-putting of narrowboats - instead high sails flap, swaying masts creak and anchors jangle.

Tall reeds that line the water's edge try to hide the views but when you reach the pub, an oasis of grassy space wins. A destination with wooden tables planted under wise spirited trees that overlook the water as if they're the custodians of sea wrecks (somehow just calling it a beer garden seems too meagre!)

It's a 'seasidey' pub and the bar tells you the tide times before you get to the taps. Hop chains dress the interior and salt-coloured wood furnishings dominate the charisma. The promise inside is of an open fire and a wood-burning stove when the weather gets too cold for you to wither in the winds outside. Grand window seats spectacularly overlook the watery views and the pub's pack of cards invites the camaraderie of a game.

Eat from the menu or tuck into something from the waterside barbeque. The food is good (don't leave without a wedge of their carrot cake) and the ale is a real treat too. All their ales come from local breweries within about 15 miles of the pub, and our tastebuds say that Devon definitely knows its stuff when it comes to brewing!

Bar staff are friendly and welcome bikes, boots, paddles and dogs. Like the Double Locks, the other pub along the Exeter Ship Canal, this is a genuinely dog-friendly pub with free-range fun, swimming, gambolling, socialising and dog chew treats from the bar.

Kids get the excitement of the estuary bank beach and space to explore or imagine wild water stories with the sea breeze in their hair.

An unforgettable pub. One you'll talk about long after you've left, and probably plan to visit again as soon as you can. One of our favourites. Amazing.

Make a day of it...

How you get here is the main part of your day out. Walk, bike, go by canoe, or catch the ferry.

A world without cars is barely imaginable. That is until you arrive at the Turf. It's a car-free heaven, and everyone who comes here has had to leave their 4x4 armour behind. The nearest car park is far enough away to allow you to feel isolated in a remote corner of Devon. The whole experience is about exploring the elements on foot. Walking the towpath is like a waterways expedition, with the prize ahead (the perfect pub) hidden behind the tall grass.

Catch the ferry
Start your day in the pretty estuary town of Topsham. Then catch the ferry to cruise all the way across the estuary to the Turf. It's a windy crossing on a good day, a 15-minute seafaring thrill. Return full circle at the end of the day.

Easter hols & from late May to mid September daily. Weekends only April, rest of May & September. Also available for private charter.
T:07778 370582
www.topshamtoturfferry.co.uk

Canal boat trip
The 'White Heather' is a small boat that runs 3 times a day along the Exeter Ship Canal, ferrying passengers between the Turf and the Double Locks pub. The perfect pub crawl!
T:07806 554093

Paddles and pedals
Hire a bike from the quayside at Exeter. There are all types of bikes for hire including tandems, small bikes & child seats.

The entire length of the canal is part of National Route 2 of the Sustrans National Cycle Network and is extremely easy pedalling.

Both experienced and novice canoeists can hire single and double kayaks, or open Canadian canoes. A gentle paddle to the pub and back.

There's also a bike shop & hire centre, open daily all year.
T:01392 424241
www.saddlepaddle.co.uk

Go for an amble

Face towards the sea and follow
the Exe Estuary Trail. It's a narrow
path curling dramatically round
the edge of the estuary leaving the
Turf behind in its dynamic setting.
The estuary is a designated Site of
Special Scientific Interest (SSSI), a
Special Protected Area (SPA) and
a wetland site of special interest
(Ramsar), due to the wealth of
wildlife living here. You might even
see avocets feeding on the mud flats
at low tide (with that in mind, we
had to try the Exeter's Avocet guest
ale, Devon's only organic real ale,
served at the pub. A locally brewed
ale that's pale and delicious!)

Come in summer or winter

Guesses are that it may be a crueller
destination in winter since the pub
is only fully open from March to
October, but on a summer day
it's like a carefree escape to a mini
wilderness on the edge of the tides.

Pub nitty-gritty

The Turf
Exeter Canal
Exminster
Devon
EX6 8EE
T:01392 833128
www.turfpub.net

Opening hours

Open all day every day April - Sept. Winter opening times vary. Best to check with the pub first.

Food

Daily 1200 - 1430 (Sat & Sun 1500) & 1900 - 2100 (Sat 2130). No food Sun eve. Locally sourced, imaginative home-made food. BBQ area outside when weather good. Veggie options.

Drink

Freehouse

Permanent ales: All local real ales including Otter's Ale & Bitter, O'Hanlons Yellowhammer Ale.

Guest ales:
Always from local breweries within about 15 miles of the pub, including Exeter's Avocet organic Ale & Exeter's Ferryman.

Other drinks:
One of their lagers and two of their wines are local and they also sell locally produced cider and apple juice.

Other essentials

Dog-friendly - yes, yes and yes! (we didn't spot Poppy, the pub dog when we were there - we look forward to meeting her next time)

Real fires

GONGOOZLING

It's a triangular beer garden surrounded on all sides by wild water.

TIP

When we first visited the Turf, we couldn't find a sign for the 'Ladies', but eventually opened the door labelled 'Mermaids'. The loos allowed enough space for the slim scales of fish maidens but it was a tight squeeze for us!

Thankfully for the 2010 season, the Turf has put in brand new toilets, with twice the space.

Stay over

Backpackers can ask at the bar and usually pitch their tent in the pub garden perched on the water's edge between the estuary and the canal.

THE DAY IN A NUTSHELL

A pub location with wow factor. And the blessing is you can't get there by car.

Location

OS Grid ref: SX963860

Canal: **Exeter Ship Canal, by Turf Lock**

OS Explorer Map: **110/114**

How to get there

By train
Nearest station is Starcross (2 miles from Turf)
or Exeter stations (approx 5 miles)
National Rail Enquiries T:08457 484950

By bus
Traveline T:0871 2002233

By car
One of only a few pubs in the UK which can't
be reached by car (nearest parking ½-mile).

By boat
The White Heather ferry from Double Lock pub
to Turf Lock, 3 times a day.
T:07806 554093

Topsham Turf Ferry from Topsham to the
Turf. Daily Easter hols & from late May to
mid September, weekends April, rest of May
& September. Available for private charter.
T:07778 370582 www.topshamtoturfferry.co.uk

Moorings
The canal above the lock and pub is often two-
abreast with boats and yachts on both sides.
Canoes can be taken out of the water, and
relaunched, by the pub just next to the lock.

Local Tourist info

Quay House Visitor Centre
T:01392 271611 www.exeter.gov.uk

Exeter town website
www.exeter.gov.uk

Telford Inn
Llangollen Canal

On a day out at the Pontycysyllte Aqueduct, you can snatch lunch and a pint in the pub, but nothing is going to distract you from the real point of coming here. The aqueduct is the showpiece of Britain's inland waterways. A World Heritage site. A marvel of engineering and a jaw-dropping piece of living history. Sightseers arrive wide-eyed and leave humbled.

The Llangollen Canal ambles 46 miles, crossing the scenic north-east corner of Wales, yet once carried industrial materials of coal, limestone, clay and ironstone on their way to the Midlands. It was built by William Jessop and Thomas Telford over 200 years ago, climbing the contours of the landscape through locks and tunnels. When the Dee Valley got in the way, ordinary mortals would have admitted defeat, but Thomas Telford had his own ideas. He decided to make the canal fly through the air, 127 feet above the river valley.

The Pontycysyllte is often described as a bath-tub carrying narrowboats in the sky. Spanning 1007 feet, 19 arches (and fresh air) have held up the cast-iron trough since the aqueduct first opened in 1805. The piers remain as they were when first built, unnervingly still standing with masonry joints fixed by a concoction of lime and ox blood. And the ironwork of the canal trough is sealed by a quirky potion of Welsh flannel and lead dunked in boiling sugar.

Narrowboats cross in single file with only a slither of space starboard or portside, and pale-faced drops that haven't been spoiled by safety railings. There's a slim towpath, hugging the water with a sheer drop to the one side. The towpath was originally for horses pulling narrowboats, and if you look closely at the railings you can see the grooves made by repeated rubbing of ropes.

Nowadays, the path boldly asks visitors on foot if they are brave enough to cross. Many, quivering, will say "yes!" and many resign at the edge. For the brave it's an unrivalled experience, walking high with swallows and stocky dreams of the great industrialists of a bygone era.

The nearest pub is a good place to sit and chat about the Pontcysyllte (it's probably best not to try pronouncing Pontcysyllte in public, until the pub has oiled your tongue). The aptly named Telford Inn is situated in Trevor Basin, only a few hundred yards away. The pub building was previously known as Scotch Hall and is believed to have been built at the same time as the canal by the Ellesmere Canal Company (probably for the supervising engineer working on the aqueduct).

The pub overlooks the basin and has seating outside to make the best of its waterside position. In summer it reliably gets packed and the outside seating area becomes sardine-full.

The Telford Inn might not necessarily win our vote for number 1 best pub on the canals, but if it's about location, this pub is definitely prizeworthy. You'll go away well-fed, well-watered, and raving about the Ponty.

Make a day of it...

Pontcysyllte Aqueduct

It's listed as one of the 7 Wonders of the Waterways. Pontcysyllte Aqueduct is the longest and highest in the UK. Built by William Jessop and Thomas Telford, it's considered to be one of Telford's greatest engineering achievements. The aqueduct and 18km of canal were awarded World Heritage Site status in 2009.

If you decide to risk walking the most vertiginous towpath in Britain, you'll probably discover it's the longest short walk you've ever known. Whatever you do, don't stop halfway across and question the physics and fresh air that hold you up (the reality is too unnerving). It's an overblown experience tapping all of the senses.

When you reach the other side, you could follow the road down to the river and get the awesome view from below. (It's a steep hill back up to the Basin though).

British Waterways info centre in Trevor Basin - Pontcysyllte Infomation Point Open Easter - November Daily inc Bank Hols 1030 - 1730

Trevor Basin

During the Industrial Revolution, Trevor Basin was a busy wharf with tramways linked to iron foundries, chemical works, brick and tile works and the nearby coal mines.

It is busy today with holiday and trip boats, and as Anglo Welsh Waterway Holidays have one of their bases here, there is usually plenty of boating activity to watch.

Boat trips across the aqueduct

Hop on 'Jones the Boats' and enjoy a 45-minute cruise over the aqueduct and back, with a cuppa or something stronger.

Narrowboat 'Eirlys' cruises across the aqueduct from Easter to the end of October.

Daily May - Aug & in school hols Apr, Sept & Oct. Rest of season only Sat & Sun. Departures 1200, 1300, 1400 and 1500. Booking advised.
Charter trips also available.

T:01691 690322
www.canaltrip.co.uk

Boat trip from Llangollen

A 2-hour canal cruise aboard the 'Thomas Telford' to the aqueduct from Llangollen Wharf.

Easter to October Daily 1215 & 1400. Booking available from 2 weeks prior.
T:01978 860702
www.horsedrawnboats.co.uk

Pub nitty-gritty

Telford Inn
Station Road
Trevor
Llangollen
Clwyd
LL20 7TT
T:01978 820469

Opening hours

Sat - Sun & daily in summer hols 1100 - 2300.
Rest of year Mon - Fri 1100 - 1500 & 1800 - 2300.

Food

Daily 1100 - 2300 spring and summer.
Winter Mon - Fri 1200 - 1430 & 1800 - 2130,
Sat - Sun all day. Good choice of traditional
pub food. They try to source all produce
locally. If you want to eat inside in their
restaurant, it's a good idea to book in the
summer as it gets so busy. Veggie options.

Drink

Freehouse.

Permanent ales: **Real ale isn't a priority for the
pub, but in the tourist season there is usually
at least one ale.**

Other essentials

Dog-friendly but must be kept on a lead.

Wheelchair access

Real fires

GONGOOZLING

Large outdoor space with plenty of tables so you can gongoozle the boating activity to your heart's content.

TIP

Understandably, the Aqueduct is a world-renowned attraction for tourists.

The pub can get extraordinarily busy in summer so if you want a good chance of grabbing a seat outside, it's best to avoid weekends and Bank Holidays if you can.

THE DAY IN A NUTSHELL

The Ponty!!

Location

OS Grid ref: **SJ270422**

Canal: **Llangollen Canal, in Trevor Basin**

OS Explorer Map: **256**

How to get there

By train
Nearest station is Chirk
National Rail Enquiries T:08457 484950

By bus
Traveline Cymru T:0871 2002233

By car
Public car park for Pontcysyllte on the opposite side of the canal to the pub

By boat
'Eirlys', Jones the Boats
Trevor Basin. Public trips across the aqueduct.
Daily Easter to Oct. Charter also available.
T:01691 690322 www.canaltrip.co.uk

Anglo Welsh Waterway Holidays
Trevor Basin. Holiday & day boat hire.
T:0117 3041122 www.anglowelsh.co.uk

'Thomas Telford'
Llangollen Wharf. Boat trips to the aqueduct.
Daily Easter to Oct.
T:01978 860702 www.horsedrawnboats.co.uk

Moorings
There are no moorings in the Basin but there are moorings along the canal between Pontcysyllte and Llangollen (apart from the narrow winding areas) and on the other side of the aqueduct towards Chirk.

Local Tourist info

Llangollen Tourist Information Centre
T:01978 860828 llangollen@nwtic.com

Llangollen website
www.llangollen.org.uk

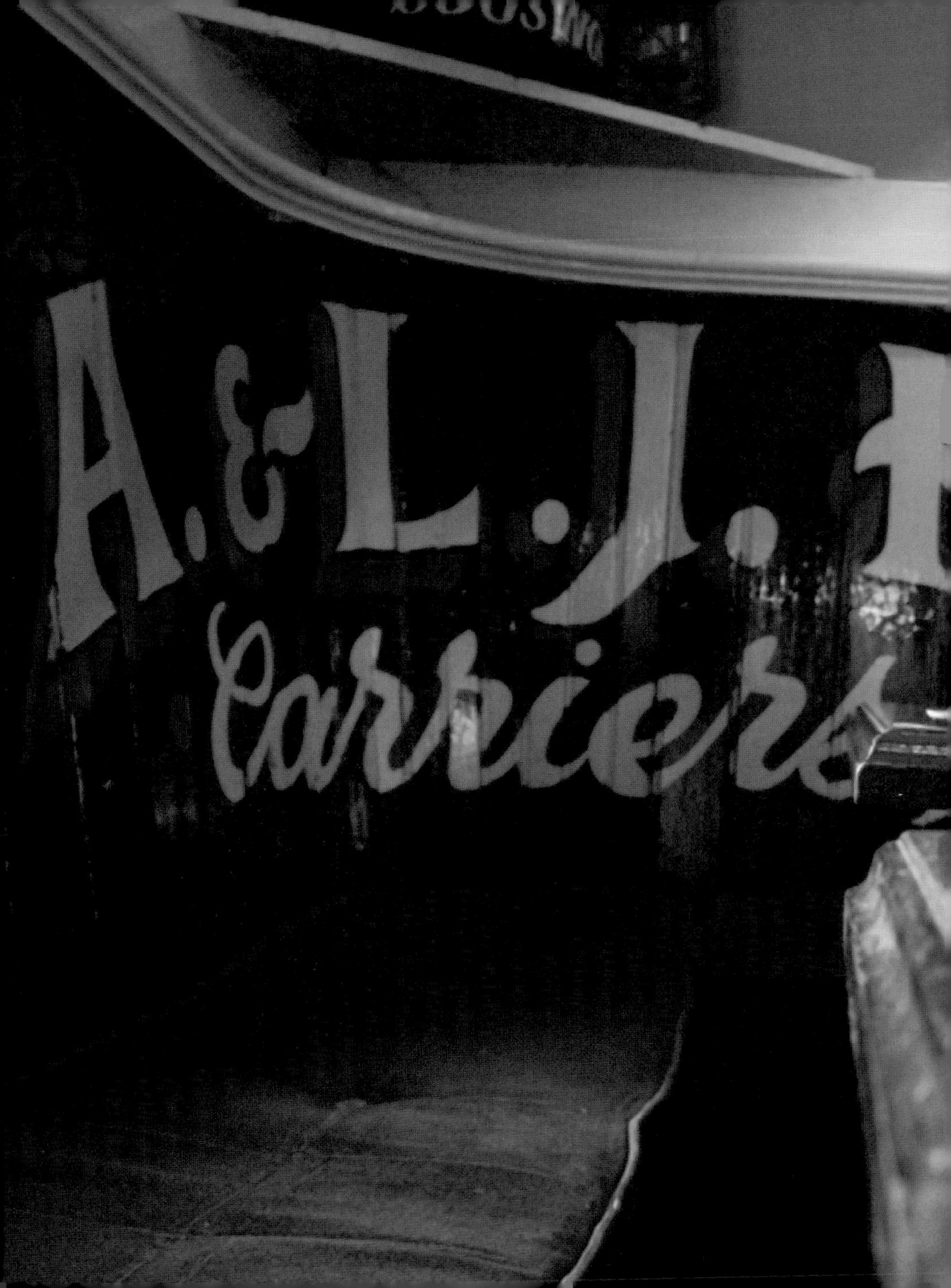
A.&L.J.
Carriers

Navigation
Peak Forest Canal

You won't see a beehived sassy woman fagging it behind the bar today but, for ITV's Corrie fans, this is the place to go and reminisce over a G and T because it was no less than Elsie Tanner (alias Pat Phoenix) who owned the pub in the late 1960s.

The day we called in we were greeted by as feisty a smile as Elsie herself could have managed and warmly invited to taste the beers before we chose which one to have.

If you didn't know better, you'd say the décor was gaudy – but this is a canal pub through to its heart. So an overdose of lurid red, green and yellow swirls is utterly appealing, even down to the roses and castles painted on an otherwise ordinary mop and bucket propped nonchalantly in the bar.

The designated eating and bar areas aren't starchily separated, so you always comfortably know you're in a pub not a restaurant. The alfresco-minded can sit outside and, although you can't quite see the water from the tables and chairs provided, the ambience still tries to imagine the former canal hubbub.

The pub was built at the same time as the canal and lives with a 'hotpot' of yesterday's stories.

Bugsworth Basin was built in the 1790s and became one of the busiest in Britain. Horse-drawn carts would haul limestone down inclined planes to load into waiting narrowboats. The Navigation is by the Upper Basin, and there is a network of bridges, basins and canal arms which give some indication of how important a hub this area once was.

Sitting with peaceful views of green countryside makes it a cerebral challenge to connect with the nitty-gritty behind the heritage of this place. The basin once played a key role in the deluge of stone quarries and limekilns and the inevitable scarring that the Industrial Revolution stamped on the land.

There's something about this pub that makes it stand out from the crowds. Most pub landlords and landladies like to claim their establishment has good atmosphere, but in this pub the character blows its own trumpet, dominating the experience of your visit.

Stories and memorabilia fill the walls, the signwritten names of canal companies liven up the seats and bags of character make the Navigation unique.

Make a day of it...

Bugsworth Basin

The route to Bugsworth Basins was once the main line of the Peak Forest Canal. In their heyday, the Basins made the largest inland waterway port ever created, so large that it was possible for 100 boats to be moored there at the same time. Derbyshire limestone, brought down from the hills by tramway, was loaded onto waiting boats at the canal terminus.

Because of its location, the Peak Forest Tramway remained the most efficient means of transporting the stone down from the hills, so it was not until the 1920s, with improved rail and road links, that the tramway finally fell silent. After the Basins went into decline, the canal's main line was switched to what had once been the branch to Whaley Bridge.

The Basins have been restored thanks to the efforts over 3 decades by volunteers of the Inland Waterways Protection Society (IWPS), and are now a Scheduled Ancient Monument.

www.brocross.com/iwps

Bugsworth or Buxworth?

This small village has changed name several times. Starting life in the 1200s as 'Buggesworth', by the 1600s it had become 'Bugsworth'. Some people found the name offensive and succeeded in getting the village name finally changed to 'Buxworth' in 1930. (You'll notice that the Basins have kept their original spelling).

A towpath amble

Follow the towpath down below the steep stone sides of the Basin. It's only about a mile along the canal towpath, beyond the junction with the main line of the canal, to Whaley Bridge. You can also trek up the hill opposite the pub along the original route of the tramways.

Go boating

See the Basins from the viewpoint of the working boatmen. Hire a boat for the day from Whaley Bridge and cruise the quiet waters along the picturesque Peak Forest Canal to the Lower, Middle and Upper Basins. Moor below the pub, then after a hearty lunch, enjoy a slow cruise back to Whaley Bridge.

Available all year for up to 8 hours. April - Oct 0900 - 1700. Nov - Mar 0900 - dusk.
T:01663 747808
www.trafalgarmarineservices.co.uk

Sweets

THE NAVIGATION INN

HOW TO ORDER YOUR FOOD — IN THE PUB

Select from our MENU or our SPECIALS boards.

CHOOSE A TABLE AND ORDER AND PAY FOR YOUR FOOD AT THE BAR giving your table number where possible.

Or if you prefer our STAFF will find you a table in our **RESTAURANT** with full **WAITRESS SERVICE.**

Enjoy your meal.

Pub nitty-gritty

Navigation Inn
Brookside
Buxworth
High Peak
Derbyshire
SK23 7NE
T:01663 732072
www.navigationinn.co.uk

Opening hours

Daily 1100 - midnight.

Food

Daily 1100 - 2300 spring and summer.
Winter Mon - Fri 1200 - 1430 & 1800 - 2130
Sat - Sun all day. (Breakfasts for early birds).
Good choice of traditional home-made pub
food. Veggie options.

Drink

Freehouse

Permanent ales: Timothy Taylor's Landlord,
Robinson's Unicorn.

Guest ales: 3 floating ales, including
Theakston's Old Peculier. Also many from
local and micro breweries.

Other essentials

Very dog-friendly

Wheelchair access (ramp to main entrance)

Real fires

B&B rooms

GONGOOZLING
Large outdoor space with
plenty of tables

TIP
Every year, Buxworth
village has well-dressing
ceremonies in winter and
early summer. It's a village
affair getting ready for
the ceremonies, designing
boards decorated with
flower petals.

The Navigation becomes
a hive of activity and if
you time your visit right,
you could watch the well
dressers in action.

THE DAY IN A NUTSHELL
Rural Derbyshire's secret
industrial history.

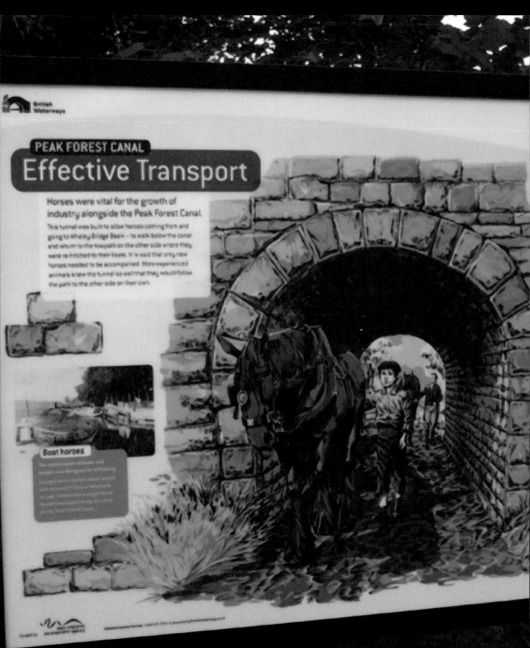

PEAK FOREST CANAL
Effective Transport

Horses were vital for the growth of
industry alongside the Peak Forest Canal.

This tunnel was built to allow horses coming from and
going to Whaley Bridge Basin – to walk below the canal
and return to the towpath on the other side where they
were re-hitched to their boats. It is said that only new
horses needed to be accompanied. More experienced
animals knew the tunnel so well that they would follow
the path to the other side on their own.

Boat horses

The illustration of a horse and
harness are being used to show
the physical input of horses needed
along the canal. Peak Forest
Canal is now a place of recreation.

Location

OS Grid ref: SK023820

Canal: Peak Forest Canal, in Bugsworth Basin

OS Explorer Map: OL1

How to get there

By train
Nearest station is Whaley Bridge
National Rail Enquiries T:08457 484950

By bus
Traveline T:0871 2002233

By car
Pub car park

By boat
'Phoenix' is a day boat for hire from Whaley
Bridge. T:01663 747808
www.trafalgarmarineservices.co.uk

Judith Mary II, a restaurant boat which runs
trips from Whaley Bridge, was once visited by
Princess Diana. Charter trips also available.
T:01663 732408

Moorings
There are moorings in the Basin and along the
canal arm between the Basin and the main
Peak Forest Canal.

Local Tourist info

Tourist Information Centre
Nearest is Buxton.
T:01298 25106 tourism@highpeak.gov.uk
www.visitpeakdistrict.com

Inland Waterways Protection Society (IWPS)
Set up in 1968 to work (successfully!) towards
the eventual restoration of Bugsworth Canal
Basin. The Society's current aims are to
secure its long-term future.
www.brocross.com/iwps

The Weighbridge
Worcester & Birmingham Canal

Approaching the front door of a tiny intimate pub in a village could send ricochets of dread into the first-time visitor not knowing what awkwardness awaits the other side of that door. The locals might stare, or worse still collectively inhale if anyone dares to sit down in the seat Old Ted has sat in for the last fifty years (and he'll be here again to sit in it, today, on the dot, in four minutes).

Forget the fear when you arrive in Alvechurch; just barge into the Weighbridge and plonk yourself wherever you like. Inside there are three tiny rooms with nose-rubbing budge-up intimacy. The licensees, John and Jane, can be blamed for the success of the pub and the locals are notoriously friendly too.

John's beer is as delicious as Jane's food and, by no coincidence, the local CAMRA group congregates here. In fact, anyone and everyone seems to congregate here: it's popular with locals and boaters - and even Morris men leaping with accordions of merriment regularly turn up for a pint and a dance at the Weighbridge.

The pub's friendly atmosphere is backed up with real ales as good as the specially made Tillerman's Tipple and Bargee's Bitter.

Check before you go if you want a quiet drink, because throughout the year the Weighbridge holds busy Beer Festivals. These have become an institution around these parts drawing large crowds for a minuscule pub.

Its popularity has forced the pub to burst out of its brick skin into a partially gazebo-covered beer garden adjacent to Alvechurch Marina.

When you sit in the beer garden today, overlooking the marina, you won't see many working boats turn up, but the Weighbridge pub was once the old Weighbridge office for unloading coal from barges onto horses and carts for local deliveries.

Today, Alvechurch is the home of one of the largest narrowboat hire fleets in the country, so throughout the boating season there's plenty to watch as holidaymakers set off joyously (and often clumsily with 'L' plated tillers), and others return reluctantly (proficient 2-week veterans).

Anyone who visits the Weighbridge has to love it for its great beer, great food and the friendliest of welcomes.

Make a day of it...

Alvechurch village

Alvechurch may be only a short hop from Birmingham but it has all the credentials of a village - four pubs and a church on the hill overseeing the community.

The marina

Alvechurch Marina is the base for one of the UK's largest holiday narrowboat hire companies, Alvechurch Waterways Holidays. There are narrowboats to look at of course, and dream of that glorious 2-week water break. The small shop is packed with canal books and intriguing bits and bobs of chandlery (boating paraphernalia).

Towpath amble

From the pub, turn right, go over the bridge then head down to the towpath.

Turn right to go under the bridge and past moorings to the edge of the village and another canalside pub, the Crown Inn.

Alternatively, head left past the marina, and follow the towpath round into glorious countryside.

Morris dancing

Alvechurch is world-renowned for its boats, but the locals know it for Morris men too. The Weighbridge's beer festivals are a great excuse for leaping men, strangely dressed, with bells on their ankles and a sparkle in their eyes.

And turn up early on New Years' Day to join the gathering crowds at the Crown Inn just along the canal from the Weighbridge. The Alvechurch Morris Mumming Play is a tradition at the Crown; music, clonking sticks, kicking and hopping, smiles and beer to boot.
www.alvechurchmorris.org.uk

Hire a boat for the day

Anglo Welsh Waterways Holidays have a base at Tardebigge, a short distance from Alvechurch. Their base is just the other side of the tunnel leading to the famous Tardebigge Locks (the longest lock flight in Britain).

Hire a boat and head towards Alvechurch for a gentle cruise.
Boat hire from 0900 - 1600 during the main season (winter 0900 - 1500). Includes full tuition.
T:0117 3041122 www.anglowelsh.co.uk

Pub nitty-gritty

The Weighbridge
Scarfield Wharf
Alvechurch
Worcestershire
B48 7SQ
T:0121 4455111
www.the-weighbridge.co.uk

Opening hours

Daily 1200 - 1500 (Sat & Sun in season 1600)
& 1900 - 2300 (Sun 2230)

Food

Thu - Mon 1200 - 1400 & 1900 - 2100 (Tues
- Wed snacks only). Breakfasts are also
available during the season, Thu - Mon, by
prior arrangement. Good choice of imaginative
fresh home-cooked food with a regularly
changing menu. Veggie options.

Drink

Freehouse.

Permanent ales: Weatheroak's Tillerman's
Tipple (brewed specially for the Weighbridge),
Kinver Bargee's Bitter.

Guest ales: Two regularly changing guest ales,
including local breweries such as Purity.

Other drinks: Regularly changing real cider &
perry pump.

Other essentials

Dogs allowed in covered areas outside

Wheelchair access

Real fires

The Weighbridge holds a Beer Festival twice a
year, in May and October.

GONGOOZLING

The pub has a large beer
garden and if you walk
past the entrance to
Alvechurch Boats' office,
there are a few tables right
on the water's edge by the
marina full of boats.

TIP

The pub is too small to
have toilets inside - they're
nearby in the marina.

The Weighbridge seems
to collect awards for a
pastime - it's been voted
Pub of the Year by the
regional CAMRA groups
for the past few years, was
voted Best Waterside Pub
by Waterscape.com, and
is in the Top 6 Canalside
Pubs on Canalguide.co.uk.

THE DAY IN A NUTSHELL

A place to dream about
hiring your holiday boat
- or book it while you're
there!

Location

OS Grid ref: **SP021721**

Canal: **Worcester & Birmingham Canal, by Alvechurch Marina**

OS Explorer Map: **220**

How to get there

By train
Alvechurch (a few hundred yards away!)
National Rail Enquiries T:08457 484950

By bus
Traveline T:0871 2002233

By car
Pub car park and overspill into the car park for Alvechurch Waterway Holidays.

By boat
Alvechurch Waterway Holidays are based in the marina. Holiday boat hire.
T:0330 3330590 www.alvechurch.com

Moorings
There's plenty of mooring on the opposite side of the canal to the pub, apart from on the bank directly opposite the hireboats.

Local Tourist info

Bromsgrove Tourist Information Centre
T:01527 831809

Worcester Birmingham Canal Society
Formed in 1969, the Society still plays an important role in conserving and improving the canal. They also hold monthly meetings, usually with a visiting speaker on varied waterways-related topics, which non-members are very welcome to attend.
www.wbcs.org.uk

The Swan
Trent & Mersey Canal

Ingrained British manners say 'it's rude to stare' – but not when you're at Fradley Junction. Everyone's a gongoozler here. It's a place for shameless gawping and it's possibly even rude not to appreciate the prowess and antics of narrowboats pottering past.

The Swan Inn sits right in the middle of the action on the junction between the Coventry Canal and the Trent & Mersey Canal. In summer, get there early enough to grab the best outdoor seat on the waterside: keep your glass full and expect an eccentric day.

On our visit we had only just taken our first sip of the guest ale, a delicious pint of Piddle Express, when a yellow vintage sports car pulled up with a verging-on-vintage cowboy at the driving wheel wearing a brown suede hat. The cowboy joined us at our table for a chat and whiled away a typically chilled waterways moment until his cider glass was empty.

That's the way it is at the Swan. You won't want to hog a table to yourself – the ambience is infectious and this is one of those canal pub gems that preserve British sociability. Cyclists, walkers, boaters, locals, motorists and caravanners from the nearby site make the Swan an eclectic hub.

Tracey the landlady is no-fuss-friendly, just like her pub. Inside the Swan is everything you want a real canal pub to be and Tracey brags she has 'no plans to modernise'. An open fire atmosphere with gloriously dark tiny rooms leading into each other, loud canalia and a splattering of loudly signwritten seats.

Order some food and you won't get designer-square plates with Picasso-drizzled jus, but you can get your gnashers into a good Boatman's Platter with a chopped up tommy, some lettuce, a satisfying white roll, a few giant wedges of tasty cheddar and a dash of no-nonsense Branston. And it's dirt cheap.

If you stay until dark, watch out for the lady ghost who reputedly appears in the mirror in the bar. But we're not fooled, this pub couldn't be spooky if it tried: besides, any real ghost worth its salt would probably only want a bag of crisps and a pint and to be as sociable as everyone else.

JUNCTION SHOP

GIFTWARE · GROCERIES
SWEETS · ICE CREAM
SMALL CHANDLERY

BRITISH WATERWAYS
NATURE RESERVE

BRITISH WATERWAYS
SHOP, CAFE &
INFORMATION CENTRE

Make a day of it...

Fradley Junction

Some people bring deckchairs to Fradley with no intention of moving a muscle all day. Why would they want to when there's so much to stare at.

'What is this life if, full of care, we have no time to stand and stare?' (WH Davies).

Fradley forces you to have time to stand and stare: it's a rare place that's so full of people and yet only busy with laziness. So many people, so chilled, all at one time.

The Swan sits right in front of the Trent & Mersey's junction with the Coventry Canal, and is in the middle of a flight of 5 locks.

Fradley Pool

An award-winning nature reserve, just below Junction Lock. It's in the British Waterways' Top Ten places to spot wildlife, so you're bound to see something interesting. Just keep your eyes open! The reserve has a bird hide, pond-dipping platforms by the pool and tree sculptures.

Towpath amble

The towpath is wide and well maintained with a good surface for wheels as far as Shadehouse Lock at the top of the lock flight. Bikes, pushchairs, wheelchairs and moto-scooters all make the most of it.

Head right out of the pub to wander up the last two locks, past the teashop by the caravan site. Or head left and across the bridge over Junction Lock to have afternoon tea at the British Waterways café (with cake to die for!). Browse for souvenirs, canal books, honey and fridge magnets in the shop and information centre.

Gongoozling

It's an unforgivingly tight turn with a 90° bend from the Coventry Canal into the lock on the Trent & Mersey Canal. Road rage is rare on the canals, but this junction cavorts with every tillerman's emotions, bringing out either wilful skills or magnificent embarrassment over tricky manoeuvres. Either way, gongoozlers are entertained. (Notice the crash marks on the canal edge in front of the pub).

Pub nitty-gritty

Swan Inn
Fradley Junction
Near Alrewas
Staffordshire
DE13 7DN
T:01283 790330
www.theswanatfradley.co.uk

Opening hours

Mon - Fri 1100 - 2300, Sat 1100 - midnight,
Sun 1200 - 2230.

Food

Mon - Sat 1200 - 1430 & 1730 - 2100 Sun
1200 - 1500 (carvery) & 1800 - 2100. Good
choice of fresh home-made pub food including
grills, fish, baguettes & rolls.Children's menu.
Veggie options.

Drink

Freehouse.

Permanent ales: Black Sheep Ale, Greene
King Abbot Ale, and 'Mucky Duck', specially
brewed by Quartz Brewing for the Swan.

Guest ales: Regularly rotating guest ales.

Other drinks:
Range of bottled ciders and occasionally they
have a cask cider.

Other essentials

Dogs are very welcome in the pub (the Swan
has two resident dogs) and if the scattered
water bowls provided didn't give you a clue
to how welcome dogs are, counting the
extraordinary number of wagging tails up and
down the towpath should.

Wheelchair access

Real fire

Children are not allowed in the bar.

GONGOOZLING

One of the best
gongoozling spots on the
canal networks. The pub
has a direct view of the
Coventry Canal's junction
with the Trent & Mersey,
and is between two
locks. Boats and people
everywhere.

TIP

Don't get confused if you
hear folks calling the pub
the 'Mucky Duck'. You're
not in the wrong place,
it's just an affectionate
nickname.

Some of the traditional
canal art decorations
in the bar of the Swan
are the work of Jackie
Burton, the previous
landlady. You might catch
her with her pots and
paintbrushes next door at
the rear of the shop.
T:01283 791974

THE DAY IN A NUTSHELL

A gongoozler's heaven.

Location

OS Grid ref: **SK140140**

Canal: **Trent & Mersey Canal, at the junction with the Coventry Canal**

OS Explorer Map: **245**

How to get there

By train
Nearest station is Lichfield
National Rail Enquiries T:08457 484950

By bus
Traveline T:0871 2002233

By car
British Waterways car park (charge)

By boat
Swan Line Cruisers
Fradley Junction. Day boat hire.
T:01283 790332
Anglo Welsh Waterways Holidays
Great Haywood. Holiday and day boat hire.
T:0117 3041122 www.anglowelsh.co.uk

Moorings
There are good 48-hour visitor moorings
between Junction Lock and Keepers Lock, just
opposite the café.

Local Tourist info

The Heart of England website
www.visittheheart.co.uk

British Waterways Visitor Centre
Fradley Junction.
T:01283 790407

Ring O' Bells
Macclesfield Canal

It's the end of the Easter hols and time to go back to school. But a bunch of Enid Blyton children are too stricken by flu so get packed off to the village of Ring O' Bells for a jolly good dose of fresh air and exercise to recover. The story goes that some queer things went on in that village... what with bells ringing mysteriously and adventures in secret passages! (Ring O' Bells Mystery by Enid Blyton 1951)

Not surprisingly, apart from its name, the Ring O' Bells pub on the Macclesfield Canal has absolutely nothing to do with Enid Blyton. But it does come with lashings of ginger beer (or real ale if you prefer) and a canal day out that includes a real-life secret passage.

From the road this pub says ordinary things, but inside there's a warm welcome lovingly knitted with canal enthusiasm. Even on a quiet day when there's plenty of choice of where to sit, this place jangles with the presence of people, and it's easy to see why it won the North West Community Pub of the Year Award in 2008 and 2009.

Beyond the hub of the bar, two adjacent snugs jest for bottoms on seats: one is called 'Sports' and the other 'Waterways'. Both are deliberately decorated for guaranteed conversation starters. The waterways room displays an impressive collection of plaques celebrating everything from IWA festivals to restoration projects. Canal maps and books, pictures on the walls and artefacts of canal art will either keep the conversation flowing, or stop it dead while you ingest.

The main bar area pays quiet homage to Ms Blyton's book, propped on a high shelf, but what grabs your eye is a row of hand bells over the bar. The ale is good: we tried one of their seasonal ales, Robinsons Dizzy Blonde, refreshingly light with a lemony tang. Don't ignore the coffee menu with 9 coffees or a warming hot chocolate in winter. Food is integrated into the bar room without compromising its character. The ethos of this pub is genuine old (but not olde) England and its pubby simplicity is its appeal. It doesn't need to pretend to be more than a local boozer, and every stranger is welcome. We get the feeling that if any Blyton child did happen to travel by in a boat, now they're over 18, they'd love it here.

Go off exploring from the pub and take a walk down Marple Locks where you'll find the secret passage halfway up the flight. As the canal climbs the landscape through the locks, beside the water a tiny arched tunnel, cobbled underfoot, once led the horses that towed working boats. Look closer and tucked next to the edge of the lock you'll find an even tinier tunnel for the boatman. Climb down into the dark spiralling passage to meet the water as it cascades from the lock gates above. With only space for one in the passage, your imagination runs riot knowing over 200 years ago this was all in a day's work for a boatman taking cargo along the Peak Forest Canal. Working in perfect harmony, man, horse and boat split momentarily at one lock then, reunited, travelled on to the next. Britain's museums have their place, but this is the real thing!

ROBINSON'S

RING O' BELLS

Welcome to
The Peak Forest
Canal

T 01942 405070

Make a day of it...

Marple Locks

A flight of 16 locks heads away from Marple Junction through the woods towards Marple Aqueduct. Both the lock flight and the aqueduct are Grade I-listed, and the locks are among the deepest in the country, with each lock raising the canal 13 feet.

Views over Marple locks are coloured in by Peak Forest greens, stone walling and buildings that shape the character of this historic trade route.

Look out for Possett Bridge, by lock 13. It acquired its name because Samuel Oldknow, a local industrialist and promoter of the canal, was anxious that the canal should be finished on time. In a bid to spur on the navvies working on the canal, he had 'ale possetts' (hot milk, ale, bread & spice) made for their breakfast by the nearby Navigation Inn. The plan must have worked: the canal was completed in time for Oldknow's boat to make the first trip through the locks.

Also look out for Samuel Oldknow's warehouse by lock 9.

Marple Aqueduct

At the foot of Marple Locks, the 300ft-long aqueduct took nearly 7 years to complete and stands over 100ft above the River Goyt below. If that's not dramatic enough, the railways stormed in and overshadowed the canal with an even higher railway viaduct alongside.

Marple Junction

The Ring O' Bells is near the end of the Macclesfield Canal. Turn right onto the towpath to reach Marple Junction, where the Macclesfield meets the Peak Forest Canal.

One of the most impressive lock keeper's 'cottages' on the canals sits on the juntion. It was built by Samuel Oldknow and it is popularly believed that its first owner was the manager of the boat-building yard next door. The house is now owned by the Allcard family who run a training centre, including boat handling courses, at the boatyard. www.toplocktraining.co.uk

Pub nitty-gritty

Ring O' Bells
130 Church Lane
Marple
Stockport
Cheshire
SK6 7AY
T:0161 4272300
www.ringobellsmarple.co.uk

Opening hours

Daily 1200 - midnight.

Food

Mon - Thu 1730 - 2000. Fri - Sun 1200 - 2030.
Good choice of locally sourced home-made
pub food. Veggie options.

Drink

Robinsons Brewery pub

Permanent ales: Robinsons Unicorn Best
Bitter & Hatters Mild.

Guest ales: 5 seasonal ales.

Other drinks:
Good wine list and long coffee menu.

Other essentials

Dog-friendly

Wheelchair access

Real fire

One of the pubs on the 'Marple Real Ale Trail'

GONGOOZLING

The pub has a patio,
filled with plant pots,
overlooking the canal.

TIP

Come in mid September
during the Marple Food &
Drink Festival. Its motto
is 'Shop Local, Eat Fresh
food, Live Better'. The
Festival is a great excuse
to try the Marple Real Ale
Trail, and see who wins
the 'Samuel Oldknow Pie
Competition'.
marplefoodanddrinkfestival.
org.uk

Robinsons Brewery

The brewery is very much
a family affair. William
Robinson bought their
first inn in 1838, and the
brewery and pubs are now
being run by the sixth
generation of Robinsons.

THE DAY IN A NUTSHELL

An everyday pub with
the bonus of a canal
adventure for grown-up
children.

Location

OS Grid ref: SJ960883

Canal: Macclesfield Canal, by bridge 2

OS Explorer Map: 277

How to get there

By train
Marple
National Rail Enquiries T:08457 484950

By bus
Traveline T:0871 2002233

By car
Large pub car park

By boat
Braidbar Boats
Higher Poynton. Holiday boat hire.
T:01625 873471 www.braidbarboats.co.uk
Trading Post
Higher Poynton. Day hire boats.
T:01625 872277 www.canaltradingpost.co.uk

Moorings
There are limited moorings just before the
Junction, and more if you turn right on to the
Peak Forest Canal.

Local Tourist info

Tourist Information Centre
Nearest is Buxton. T:01298 25106
www.visitpeakdistrict.com

Marple Locks Heritage Society
Works in partnership with British Waterways to
promote and enhance the flight. The Society
also organises the Marple Locks Festival every
other year.
T:0161 4270803 www.marplelocks.org.uk

Marple Lock Flight
A virtual tour of the lock flight with points of
interest along the way. www.marple-uk.com

Enid Blyton Society
www.enidblytonsociety.co.uk

The George Inn

The George is a vision of Olde England in a building packed with character that can only be pasted by time not design. Priest holes, low ceilings, creaking beams, nooks and crannies and real fires to snuggle up to, give this pub special cosiness.

The building was once a 12th-century monastery, but it is the Cask Marque ale served here these days that has become a beer connoisseur's grail. The George says 'we champion small regional breweries when stocking our cellar' (and Coolcanals' taste buds can vouch that the choice from the taps is usually good). Wines, coffees or herbal teas are all served too; and the food is extremely edible, as well as reasonably priced.

The hardest thing about this pub is choosing where to sit. Tiny rooms seem to tuck themselves in every direction and just when you think you've discovered them all, another cubby-hole appears around a corner. Each space feels different with floors of wood, flagstones, tiles, carpets; and walls of stone, wood panelling or just hidden behind grandfather clocks and wall hangings.

Throughout the pub, old timber blends with new additions. The solid wood tables for eaters and drinkers are the sort your Mum might have had in her dining room when you were a kid (except these are sanded rustically in a way that would have made her squeal).

The person next to you could be a great-granny or a lycra-sprayed cyclist since the George is one of those rare pubs that effortlessly make different types of customers feel at home – "olives or crisps, Martini or Hobgoblin?" It's a friendly pub that's busy for a reason. Boaters, cyclists, unhealthy walkers like us and infernally hungry children are offered take-away fish and chips too. The pub welcomes children, but doesn't insult them with plastic 'family fun'.

The Kennet & Avon Canal running straight past the George is part of the National Cycle Network Route 4, which explains why it's a popular watering hole for bikes, boots and boats.

In the best of summer you'll have to scramble through piles of dismounted bikes propped along the waterside, to grab a patch of grass on the towpath or a table at lunchtime in the beer garden for good al-fresco eating and gongoozling.

At
The George
'British
Beef
always'
The Cattle in
our county enjoy
a diet of rich,
lush grass and
produce meat of
consistency high quality

Make a day of it...

You could spend the whole day doing nothing more than simply relaxing in the George, but there's plenty of canal highlights to explore along the towpath. So bring your bike with you, or a pair of comfy boots. If you turn right out of the pub, it's a 2-mile stroll to the Georgian city of Bath. Turn left out of the pub to visit one of the canal's pumping stations, and its grandest aqueduct.

Claverton Pumping Station

About a mile from the pub, follow the signpost down from the canal, crossing over the railway. The Pumping Station was built to pump water up from the River Avon to feed the canal. It has been restored by volunteers, and you can see it in action on special 'Pumping Days'.

Open to the public Apr 4 - Oct 24 Wed, Sat, Sun & Bank Hols.
1000 - 1700 (last admission 1630)
(Wed 1000 - 1600 last admission 15.30)

Pumping Days
Once or twice monthly during the season.
Specific dates vary.

T:01225 483001 www.claverton.org

Dundas Aqueduct

About a mile further on, the towpath crosses to the other side of the water as you approach Dundas Aqueduct. A footbridge takes you over the entrance to Brassknocker Basin (the old Somersetshire Coal Canal) before you reach the aqueduct.

Dundas Aqueduct was built in 1804 by John Rennie, chief architect and engineer of the Kennet & Avon Canal. According to the useful British Waterways' information board next to the aqueduct, Rennie wanted to use brick rather than Bath stone, because he thought stone was too expensive and not up to the job. In the end he lost the argument and stone was used anyway. Just as well, you might think, when you feast your eyes on this classic monument today!

If you look closely at the stonework, you will see the proud signatures of the stonemasons.

Pub nitty-gritty

The George Inn
Mill Lane
Bathampton
Bath
BA2 6TR
T:01225 425079
www.chefandbrewer.co.uk

Opening hours
Mon - Fri 1100 - 2300. Sat 1000 - 2300, Sun 1100 - 2230.

Food
All day. Good choice of fresh seasonal food inc grills, fish, mezze, etc. Special deals available. Veggie options.

Drink
Chef and Brewer pub

Permanent ales: Courage Best, Wells Bombardier, Greene King Old Speckled Hen, Wychwood Hobgoblin.

Guest ales: Changed weekly. Many from local breweries such as Butcombe in Bristol.

Cask Marque accredited

Other drinks: Speciality teas and coffees.

Other essentials
Dogs are allowed in outside areas only

Wheelchair access

Real fires

Live music on Saturdays and Bank Holiday weekends throughout the spring and summer.

GONGOOZLING
There are tables and chairs to the front of the pub, or you can just casually spread out along the towpath.

TIP
The Kennet & Avon Canal is immensely popular and the George can be heaving at peak times. Arrive early if you want a seat.

THE DAY IN A NUTSHELL
Busy boats, bikes, boots. Bursting bellies and beer.

Location

OS Grid ref: **ST776664**

Canal: **Kennet & Avon Canal, by bridge 183**

OS Explorer Map: **155**

How to get there

By train
Nearest train station is Bath Spa
National Rail Enquiries T:08457 484950

By bus
Traveline T:0871 2002233

By car
Pub car park

By boat
Bath Canal Boat Company
Bath. Holiday boat hire.
T:01225 312935 www.bathcanalboats.co.uk

Kennet & Avon Canal Trust
Brassknocker Basin. Boat trips.
T:01380 721279 www.katrust.org.uk

Bath Narrowboats. Day boat hire & boat trips.
T:01225 447276 www.bath-narrowboats.co.uk

Bath & Dundas Canal Co.
Brassknocker Basin.
Day boat, Canadian canoe & bike hire
T:01225 722292 www.bathcanal.com

Moorings
Long stretch of moorings just outside the pub.

Local Tourist info

Bath Tourist Information Centre
T:0844 8475256 www.visitbath.co.uk

Kennet & Avon Canal Trust
The Trust, based in Devizes has worked
tirelessly for over 40 years. Initially formed to
bring about the restoration of the Kennet &
Avon, its main objectives now are to continue
to protect, enhance and promote the canal.
T:01380 721279 www.katrust.org.uk

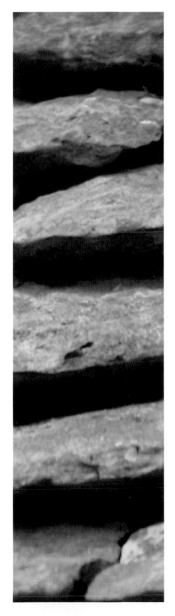

Admiral Nelson
Grand Union Canal

At first glance there's not a lot here except a sleepy village in the middle of Northamptonshire's unsung countryside. But on the quiet, Braunston is quintessential Britain, without the fanfares of tourist fame. Winding country lanes cut through fields bordered with hawthorn hedgerows. In May it's a blossom-time riot in white, with the history of Pagan weddings and festivals scattering from the region's many medieval sites.

Referred to as Brandestone in the Domesday Book, Braunston does its bit today to stay true to its village status - a teashop, idyllic stone cottages, an ancient Inn and the old bakery even hangs a 'Hovis' sign to waft imaginary smells of bread from the retired oven, baked, of course, with flour ground in the old windmill next to the church on the hill.

It all adds up to enough grand bumpkin status for any village, yet something in the air says the 'real' village of Braunston is down on the canal. It's a floating village tucked on the junction between the Grand Union and Oxford Canals.

Canals arrived in the 1700s and the junction at Braunston became one of the busiest commercial trading points linking with London. You can still see narrowboats being built in the boatyard, but the water-village now only hums with the serenity of leisure craft.

Braunston Marina is home for clusters of well-polished permanently moored narrowboats and a popular stopover for travellers passing through by water road. It's a picturesque marina with an arched iron bridge and ancient workshops all painted in white. And looking down from the hill, the spire of All Saints Church guards over the water-village. The 'Boatman's Church', as it is known, has christened, married and buried many boaters here and earned its welcoming reputation.

A short stroll along the towpath takes you to the Admiral Nelson. Navvies once swilled ale and told tales here, but now happy holiday boaters share harmlessly exaggerated stories of their day while bar staff carry platefuls of chips around with a smile.

Canalia and boaty paraphernalia don't play a big role in decorating the interior of the pub, but the hearts of boaters do. Outside, tables line the water overlooking the lock that gets busy in the summer boating season.

Braunston has plenty of canal charm, but don't come expecting entertainment on a plate. This is an escape with a taste of living-waterways today with walkers, cyclists, gongoozlers and boaters going about their own business. Braunston claims no more than to send visitors home with a dose of waterways memories and some fantastic photographs.

THE STOP HOUSE
BRAUNSTON

ORIGINALLY CONSTRUCTED IN 1796, THIS BUILDING
WAS USED FOR THE COLLECTION OF TOLLS
AND REGISTRATION OF PASSING CRAFT BETWEEN
THE OXFORD AND GRAND JUNCTION CANALS
UP TO THE END OF THE 19TH CENTURY.

IT WAS OFFICIALLY REOPENED AS A
WATERWAY OFFICE ON JULY 13TH 1990
BY THE LORD HESKETH.

Make a day of it...

Braunston Marina

The Horsley Iron Works cast-iron bridge at the marina's entrance off the canal was erected by Thomas Telford in 1834. The busy marina has mooring for up to 250 boats, buys and sells new and used boats, has two dry docks for hire and a collection of historic buildings housing everything from books & canalia to boaters' laundry facilities.

T:01788 891373
www.braunstonmarina.co.uk

The Stop House

The Stop House near the marina entrance, was built in 1796 as a toll office to collect tolls for the Oxford and Grand Junction Canals. During its life, it has been used as a British Waterways office. Now it's a small museum.

T:01908 302500

The Boat Shop

A small shop by Braunston Bottom Lock packed with a huge range of canal books, giftware, maps & guides, prints, freshly baked bread, ice creams and much more.

T:01788 891310
www.boatshopbraunston.co.uk

Braunston Tunnel

Turn left onto the towpath in front of the pub. Just past the last 3 locks up the flight, is the 2042-yard long Braunston Tunnel. Built in the 1790s by engineers William Jessop and James Barnes, the tunnel's entrance is built from beautiful red brick. Workmen dug from both ends but due to an error in the initial surveying, didn't meet up, so it has a slight s-bend in the centre. There isn't a towpath through the tunnel, but climb the steps for a lovely walk through fields above it (keep your eyes peeled for the round red-brick air vent chimney).

Braunston Turn

Turn right onto the towpath opposite the pub and stroll down through the locks to Braunston Turn. The photogenic double cast-iron bridge spans the junction where the Grand Union Canal meets the Oxford Canal.

Historic Working Boat Rally

Come at the time of the annual boat rally and it's a fiesta of traditional working boats, colourful heritage and canal enthusiam.

End of June. www.braunstonmarina.co.uk

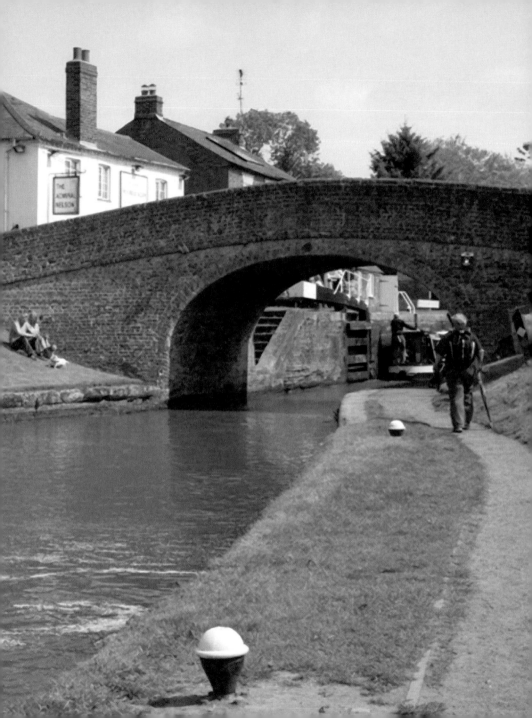

Pub nitty-gritty

The Admiral Nelson
Dark Lane
Braunston
Nr. Daventry
Northamptonshire
NN11 7HJ
T:01788 890075

Opening hours
Daily 1100 - 2300 (Sun 2230). Off season
1200 - 1500 & 1800 - 2300.

Food

All day every day in season. Off season 1200
- 1430 & 1800 - 2100. Traditional bar food.
Veggie options.

Drink

Freehouse

Permanent ales: Hook Norton's Hooky Bitter,
Black Sheep Best Bitter.

Guest ales: Seasonal ales.

Other essentials

Dogs are allowed in the bar area

Wheelchair access

Real fire

Northants skittles game in bar room

GONGOOZLING
So close to the lock, you can peer through the portholes of passing boats.

TIP
A great place to eavesdrop on holiday hireboaters at the bar recounting their day's canal stories.

Ask at the pub for the useful leaflet 'Discover Historic Braunston'. It gives circular walks with good guidance on what to look out for.

The Jurassic Way, an 88-mile trail from Banbury to Stamford, joins the canal just by the pub.

THE DAY IN A NUTSHELL
A waterways hub in the middle of rural England.

Location

OS Grid ref: **SP548659**

Canal: **Grand Union Canal, by lock 3**

OS Explorer Map: **222**

How to get there

By train
Nearest train station is Daventry
National Rail Enquiries T:08457 484950

By bus
Traveline T:0871 2002233

By car
Pub car park by the canal

By boat
Union Canal Carriers and Water Ouzel Cruises
Braunston. Holiday and day boat hire (for up to
12 passengers).
T:01788 890784
'Swan', Days Afloat
Braunston. Day boat hire or skippered cruise
for up to 12 passengers.
T:07733 010 790

Moorings
There are limited moorings up the lock flight,
but there's a longer stretch below the pub
between locks 2 and 3.

Local Tourist info

Northampton Tourist Information Centre
T:01604 838800 northampton.tic@
northamptonshireenterprise.ltd.uk

Braunston village website
www.braunston.org.uk

Waterside beer festival

River Severn, Stourport Ring

Sprawling green grass and white marquees flapping in the breeze along the waterside merely set the scene: it's the beardie enthusiasm, unhurried volunteers in uniform T-shirts and hoards of otherwise ordinary people chortling in beery passion as they gather, that make a good beer festival.

It's not only a perfect day out for kindred souls who already know the pleasures of good beer, but also the uninitiated or sceptical who'll grasp the magic of it all anyway. And the dog can come too.

Every year in mid August, Worcester holds its CAMRA Beer, Cider and Perry Festival. Arrive by train, then ignore the imposing cathedral on the skyline and follow the smaller spire of St. Andrew's church towards the racecourse where you'll find 200 real ales, 100 ciders and perries as well as delicious fruit and grape wines waiting to be quaffed, or swigged.

Most beer festivals swap your money at the entrance for a festival glass and a ream of tokens, so there's nothing as crude as paying at the bar to interrupt the experience of the day.

From here you enter a grotto of barrels: rows of tapped and labelled beer barrels leading into a vanishing point each way you look, housed charismatically under a canvas of earthy aromas.

The festival programme is the day's bible with a description of the colour, smell, flavour and strength of each ale. Nobody cares whether you choose to try something simply because it's got a weird name like 'Piddle in the Wind', or if you follow the advice of the programme to find the type of drink you might prefer.

There's usually organic beer to try and Worcester CAMRA Festival, like most beer festivals, ethically supports the best local and micro breweries.

Does life get any better than this? Laze outside on the grass or find a wooden table inside the marquee. Lie, stand, perch, mingle or huddle. When live bands play, the chatter carries on and the drinking doesn't stop.

It must be said, a good beer festival should never be about getting drunk, but rosy-cheeked-merry is fine. CAMRA, the Campaign for Real Ale, says, 'Tasting beer is just like tasting wine, but forget about spitting it out' (as if we girls would waste a drop).

More waterside festivals

National waterways boat festivals are a great day out, and usually have a well-stocked beer tent too.

Biggest festivals of the year

Crick Boat Show
Bank Holiday end of May
T:0871 7000685
www.crickboatshow.com

IWA National Festival
August. Location varies each year
T:01494 783453
www.waterways.org.uk

IWA Canalway Cavalcade
Bank Holiday beginning of May
Little Venice, London.
T:01494 783453
www.waterways.org.uk

And some of the rest

Norbury Junction Canal Festival
Bank Holiday beginning of May
Norbury Junction. Shropshire Union Canal
www.sncanal.org.uk

Skipton Waterway Festival
Bank Holiday beginning of May
Skipton. Leeds & Liverpool Canal
T:01756 795478 www.penninecruisers.com

IWA National Trailboat Festival
May. Location varies each year
T:01494 783453 www.waterways.org.uk

Etruria Canals Festival
May. Stoke-on-Trent. Trent & Mersey Canal
T:01782 233144

Historic Narrowboat Rally & Canal Festival
End of June
Braunston. Grand Union Canal
www.braunstonmarina.co.uk
T:01788 891373

Audlem Music & Art Festival
End of May
Audlem, Shropshire Union Canal
www.audlemfestival.com
T:07813 820157

Newbury Waterways Festival
End of July
Newbury. Kennet & Avon Canal
www.katrust.org

Kirkintilloch Canal Festival
August. Forth & Clyde Canal
www.kirkintillochcanalfestival.org.uk

Saltaire Festival
September
Leeds & Liverpool Canal
www.saltairefestival.co.uk

Dudley Festival of Water & Light
October
Merry Hill, Dudley No.1 Canal
www.dudley.gov.uk

More festivals on
www.coolcanalsguides.com

Worcester Festival nitty-gritty

Worcester Beer, Cider & Perry Festival

Held in mid August

Pitchcroft Racecourse
Worcester
Worcestershire
WR1 3EJ

T:08452 578975
www.worcesterbeerfest.org.uk

Location

OS Grid ref: SO842555
River: River Severn
OS Explorer Map: 204

How to get there

By train
Worcester Foregate Street
National Rail Enquiries T:08457 484950

By bus
Traveline T:0871 2002233

By car
Racecourse car park

By boat
Viking Afloat
Worcester. Holiday boat hire.
T:0845 1264098 www.viking-afloat.com

Moorings
There are visitor moorings along the river.

Local Tourist info

Worcester Tourist Information Centre
T:01905 726311
www.visitworcester.com

Worcestershire website
www.visitworcestershire.org

Canalside brewery
Kennet & Avon Canal

Ever since Britain's canals first began, they've had a close relationship with breweries. The working life of canals was thirsty work and ale houses were once scattered all across the canal networks. These days many of the small independent brewing sites on the waterside have closed down, or moved, or been gobbled up by corporatism. But, thankfully, some have held on, and and a few with visitor centres invite you to spend some time wandering arround, learning about the process of brewing, and sampling the results of course!

Wadworth's Brewery at Devizes on the Kennet & Avon Canal was founded in 1875 and is still making beer today. The brewery keeps tradition alive, selling beer in oak casks and still employing a cooper (one of only four remaining in Britain, and the only Master Cooper working exclusively on wooden beer barrels).

Because it's a working brewery, not just a museum, there's living authenticity in its Victorian corridors. If you promise not to try and steal the recipe, you can take a tour of the building and learn all about the brewing process.

In the 18th century, signwriting was a traditional skill that was as much at home on the canals as it was in the brewing industry. In the canal heyday, it was a signwriter's job to decorate the exterior panels of narrowboats with the canal company's name, write informative canal signposts, and also paint the familiar pub sign to point the way at the end of a working day.

Because navvies and boatmen generally didn't know how to read or write, the breweries hung out signs with easily recognisable images. And the Crown, the Boat, the Navigation, the Lock still feature on pub signs today. You can usually watch demonstrations of signwriting at the brewery.

A visit to a canalside brewery is bound to get you excited about the beer, but when you catch sight of the shire horses at Wadworth's, everything else slips from mind. Before the invention of fake horsepower, the brewery delivered its ales by horse and cart.

The lucky locals of Devizes still get the pleasure of seeing shires delivering ale, ciders and other drinks to the pubs daily. Visit the stables or arrive in time to watch them as they set off on their rounds. (Apparently Wadsworth's horses enjoy an occasional pint pulled into their feed, but we didn't hear that from the horse's mouth!)

After your tour there's no need to rush off because the small visitor centre has exhibitions, artefacts and memorabilia, and a shopful of souvenirs. You'll have to be strict with yourself if you don't want to go home with a set of Wadworth logos on T-shirts, mugs, teddy bears, towels, paper weights or even a bottle of beer.

The Art of Sign...

The eye-catching ...
virtually every ...
pub estate, is p...
in-house sign w...

Each sign is indi...
a high quality, ...
pleasing image ...
tone and reflec...
establishment.

The Wadworth ...
last remaining ...
departments, w...
finished letter...
of stencils or ...

WADWORTH

Make a day of it...

Brewery tours

Guided tours of the brewery are available most weekdays from the Visitor Centre. The tour takes you round the brewery building and allows time for a beer sampling session in the Visitor Centre bar.

Although the Brewery tries to include visits to the shire horses, the cooper, and a signwriting demonstration, these cannot be guaranteed as it depends upon their workload.

Tours start and end at the Visitor Centre, and last 2 hours approx.

Times of tours 1100 and 1400.
For weekends and Bank Hols, please contact Visitor Centre for availability.
Booking recommended as tours are limited.
NB Steep stairs, narrow corridors and uneven floors. Admission charge.

T:01380 723361
www.wadworth.co.uk

Shire Horses

The shire horses pull the dray around Devizes every weekday morning, delivering beer barrels to pubs within a 2-mile radius.

Their stables are open to the public
Mon-Thurs 1330-1530

The Cooper

The cooper at Wadworth's Brewery is one of only four remaining coopers in Britain. Coopering is a traditional skill, requiring craftmanship to sculpt wooden barrels from curved strips of wood. Metal hoops are hammered around the wood strips to hold them together.

Wadworth's cooper is currently the last Master Cooper in Britain, but Wadworth's Brewery is trying to secure funding to allow for an apprentice to learn his trade in order to carry it on.

Browse round the Visitor Centre

The Visitor Centre has displays about the history of Wadworth's Brewery with memorabilia and an interactive exhibition of how the brewing process works. It also offers insights into cooperage, signwriting and the shire horses.

There's a shop (where possible, the products are locally produced) and a bar to allow you to sample the beers in $\frac{1}{3}$-pint glasses (there's coffee and soft drinks too).

Wadworth Brewery nitty-gritty

Wadworth Brewery Visitor Centre
New Park Street
Devizes
Wiltshire
SN10 1JW
T:01380 732277
www.wadworth.co.uk

Opening hours

Mon - Fri 1000 - 1630,
Sat 1000 - 1600. Contact the Visitor Centre for opening times over Bank Holidays, Easter and Christmas.

Drink

Wadworth Brewery

Wadworth Brewery's ales:
Wadworth 6X, 6X Premium, JCB, Henry's Original IPA, Henry's Smooth, The Bishops Tipple, Horizon, Malt & Hops (Sept-Oct only) and Old Timer (Nov-Dec only).

Cask Marque accredited

Other drinks:
Teas, coffees and soft drinks available in the bar.

Other essentials

No dogs allowed

Wheelchair access in the Visitor Centre, though the Brewery is not suitable for wheelchairs.

Children over 12 allowed on the Brewery Tours

GONGOOZLING

The Brewery is canalside, though you'll need to follow the road round to join the towpath.

TIP

Wadworth's is only a short walk away from one of the 7 Wonders of the Waterways (see page 248). The Caen Hill flight of 16 locks climbs the hill towards Devizes.

THE DAY IN A NUTSHELL

Beer and canal heritage, all wrapped up in the same barrel.

Location

OS Grid ref: **SU001617**

Canal: **Kennet & Avon Canal, by bridge 141**

OS Explorer Map: **156**

How to get there

By train
Nearest stations are Pewsey and Chippenham
National Rail Enquiries T:08457 484950

By bus
Traveline T:0871 2002233

By car
The brewery has a car park

By boat
Devizes Marina
Devizes. Day boat hire.
T:01380 725300 www.devizesmarina.co.uk
Foxhangers Canal Holidays
By bridge 146. Holiday boat hire.
T:01380 828795 www.foxhangers.co.uk

Moorings
There's a good stretch of moorings between
bridge 141 and Devizes Wharf.

Local Tourist info

Devizes Tourist Information Centre
T:01380 729408

Devizes town website
www.devizes.org.uk

Wiltshire website
www.visitwiltshire.co.uk

More canalside breweries

Dudley No.1 Canal

Bathams Brewery.
Brierley Hill
T:01384 77229
www.bathams.co.uk

Grand Union Canal

Frog Island Brewery.
Northampton
T:01604 587772
www.frogislandbrewery.co.uk

Huddersfield Narrow Canal

Empire Brewery.
Slaithwaite.
T:01484 847343

Leeds & Liverpool Canal

Copper Dragon Brewery.
Skipton
1-hour Brewery tours Mon - Sat
1200. Booking essential.
(Evenings by special arrangement,
for groups only).
Brewery Shop & Visitor Centre.
T:01756 702130
www.copperdragon.uk.com

Saltaire Brewery.
Saltaire
Visitor Centre & brewery tours for
pre-booked groups only
Thu 1900 – 2130.
T:01274 594959
www.saltairebrewery.co.uk

Staffordshire & Worcestershire Canal

Enville Brewery.
Enville.
T:01384 873728
www.envilleales.com

Kinver Brewery.
Kinver.
T:07715 842679
www.kinverbrewery.com

Trent & Mersey Canal

Marston's Brewery.
Burton-upon-Trent
3-hour Brewery tours can be
arranged. Mon - Fri 1000, 1230 or
1400. Tues, Wed or Thu eves 1900.
All subject to availability.
T:01283 507391 / 507440
www.marstonsdontcompromise.co.uk

The National Brewery Centre.
Burton-upon-Trent
A Museum and Visitor Centre to celebrate Burton's brewing heritage. On the site of the Coors Visitor Centre & Museum of Brewing (it closed in 2008 and was formerly the Bass Museum). Open in 2010.
www.nationalbrewerycentre.co.uk

Titanic Brewery.
Burslem, Stoke-on-Trent.
Brewery tours for pre-booked groups only.
T:01782 823447
www.titanicbrewery.co.uk

Titanic Brewery
(Shugborough Estate)
Great Haywood.
Titanic brew for demonstration purposes only in a log-fired Victorian brewhouse.
Beers include 'Mi Lady's Fancy' & 'Butlers Revenge'.
T:01782 823447
www.titanicbrewery.co.uk

Monmouthshire & Brecon Canal

Breconshire Brewery. Brecon
T:01874 623731
www.breconshirebrewery.com

Shropshire Union Canal

Joule's Brewery. Market Drayton
Joule's, a renowned brewery in Stone, Staffordshire, closed down in 1974. Plans are afoot to restart the brewery in Market Drayton in 2010, on the site of the Red Lion, an original Joule's pub.
T:01630 654400
www.joulesbrewery.co.uk

Worcester & Birmingham Canal

Weatheroak Brewery.
Nr.Alvechurch
T:0121 4454411
www.weatheroakales.co.uk

Wyrley & Essington Canal

Beowulf Brewing Company.
Brownhills
T:01543 454067
www.beowulfbrewery.co.uk

Real ale rantings

We say that lagers, wines, spirits and soft drinks all have an honourable place, but whatever you drink in the pub, between glugs you'll be putting it down on a 'beer' mat. Pubs are about beer.

We're not afraid to be real ale snobs and never mince the truth when it comes to a subject as important as good beer! Our 2,000 mile canal walk is a good excuse to pop into all the canalside pubs we find dotted along the way.

And when we stumble upon the perfect combination of a cosy waterside pub with a welcoming atmosphere, serving great locally brewed ale... that's one of life's precious moments!

But what do women know about beer?

Beer hasn't always had such a hairy image. In fact, it was originally women who made beer in the home. In the earliest canalside alehouses, women simply served home-made beer from a jug. Times changed when the canals opened up transport routes connecting villages to villages, cities to cities.

Trade routes aided and abetted the Industrial Revolution and beer production got more ambitious as brewery businesses emerged. That's when the chaps took over.

Small alehouses eventually closed and commercial breweries grew bigger. Over the centuries the men grew beards and bellies as they propped up Britain's best bars. But now women are choosing to join them, even risking beer bellies as par for the course!

Blonde or dark?

One of the aims for CAMRA, the Campaign for Real Ale, is to encourage more women to try real ale, and the beer industry is keen too. Fancy-shaped glasses and campaigns promoting paler coloured beers have been used in a bid to appeal to the female drinker.

It's popularly believed in the pub industry that girls like blonde ales and boys like dark heavy brews. But we say people just like what they like. The weather, our mood, how thirsty we are, the ambience of the pub we're in, ethical and eco issues, all swing our affections to one ale or another, be they light in colour or stonkingly dark.

Our Top 10 ales

Beer appreciation is a matter of personal taste, so we don't apologise if our taste buds are out of fashion.

For us, artificially chilled trendiness can ruin the delicate after-taste that should be the lingering pleasure of a good ale; and we prefer a full pint measure, but not pulled so diligently to the brim of the glass that it tips the all-important (to us) white head into the drain.

Here's some of our favourite pints taken from our travels along the waterways:

Bathams Best Bitter
Wye Valley Hereford Pale Ale
Theakston's Old Peculier
O'Hanlon's Yellowhammer
Weatheroak's Tillerman's Tipple
Exeter's Avocet Ale (organic)
Theakston's Grouse Beater
Robinsons Ginger Tom
Purity Mad Goose
Fuller's London Porter

And then there's St Austell Tribute, Fuller's Discovery, Saltaire Blonde, Fraoch Heather Ale, Ludlow Gold, Butcombe Bitter...
And the list keeps on growing - so many lovely ales!

Real ale facts

So what is real ale?

Every part of the brewing process is important - from growing hops to how to pull a good pint. All beers start life in the same way with water, hops, malt and barley but, after the initial fermentation, bottle and keg beer is filtered and flash heated, whilst real ale is naturally cask conditioned. The yeast settles and the beer clears with the help of isinglass (the swim bladder of fish) or Irish moss (a seaweed). The beer's colour, aroma and taste vary from strong to weak, dark to pale, depending on the malt, water and hops used, and whether the cask it is sealed in is wood, steel or copper.

What is Casque Mark?

The Cask Marque Trust operates a scheme that's independent and not for profit. Pubs that join the scheme are inviting assessors to regularly drop in, unannounced, to check all their cask ales for quality (temperature, appearance, aroma and taste). If their beer passes the test, the pub gets a plaque to display. Seeing the Cask Marque logo means a good pint is assured.
www.cask-marque.co.uk

Eco tip

It's exciting on your travels to choose locally brewed real ales. Small independent breweries are constantly under threat from the onslaught of the giant 'themed' pubs, so not only does it make ethical and eco sense, it's often the best treat on offer at the bar.

CAMRA

CAMRA, the Campaign for Real Ale, is an "independent, voluntary, consumer organisation which campaigns for real ale, real pubs and consumer rights".

They work to protect local pubs and regularly lobby government on behalf of pub-goers.

They have over 100,000 members. Membership benefits include a monthly members' newspaper, quarterly members' magazine, discounted entrance to beer festivals and other regular offers.
www.camra.org.uk

101 more waterways pubs

Anchor Inn, Worcester
WHY?

Friendly, cosy tiny rooms, patio overlooking Diglis Basin.
WR5 3BW T:01905 351094

Red Lion, Cropredy
WHY?

Olde England thatch and folkie hub of Oxfordshire.
OX17 1PW T:01295 750224

Star, Stone
WHY?

Stone canal town, frequented by boaty people and narrow dogs.
ST15 8QW T:01785 813096

Angel Inn, Stourport
WHY?

Overlooks the River Severn in Stourport, the only town built specifically because of the canals.
DY13 9EW T:08721 077077

Anchor Inn, High Offley
WHY?

Rural setting and still serves beer collected in a jug from the cellar.
ST20 0NG T:01785 284569

Lock Inn, Wolverley
WHY?

Lockside view for gongoozling, good food, cosy bar room, fab canal walk.
DY10 3RN T:01562 850581

Foster's on the docks, Gloucester
WHY?

Historic docks & next door to the best waterways museum on earth.
GL1 2ES T:01452 300990

Barge Inn, Pewsey
WHY?

White horse views & camping.
SN9 5PS T:01672 851705

The Apple Cider Boat, Bristol
WHY?

Waterside cider as cool as it gets.
BS1 4SB T:01179 253560

The Boat, Penkridge
WHY?

Friendly bunch, good value food.
ST19 5DT T:01785 714174

Bridge Inn, Tibberton
WHY?

Quiet, simmering refinery, and you'll like the food.
WR9 7NQ T:01905 345874

Holly Bush Inn, Salt
WHY?

Not canalside, but thatched and beamed enough to warrant the detour, & the food is good.
ST18 0BX T:01889 508234

Bell Inn, Frampton-on-Severn
WHY?

Quintessential village pub.
GL2 7EP T:01452 740346

Stubbings Wharf, Hebden Bridge
WHY?
Good food, good beer and boat trips from the pub.
HY7 6LX T:01422 844107

Narrow Boat, Skipton
WHY?
Great atmosphere, great real ales.
BD23 1JE T:01756 797922

Tudor Arms, Slimbridge
WHY?
Good beer and across canal from Wildfowl & Wetlands Trust.
GL2 7BP T:01453 890306

The Waterway, London
WHY?
If you've got pots of money, the food looks great.
W9 2JU T:01207 2663557

Moorings Hotel
WHY?
Vantage point over Neptune's Staircase on the Caledonian Canal.
PH33 7LY T:01397 772797

The Vine, Brierley Hill
WHY?
Bathams Brewery and Black Country charisma.
DY5 2TN T:01384 78293

Sun Inn, Trevor
WHY?
Fab views over Llangollen Canal and the River Dee valley.
LL20 8EG T:01978 860651

The Canalhouse, Nottingham
WHY?
Canal running through the pub.
NG1 7EH T:01159 555060

Water Witch, Lancaster
WHY?
Real ales & continental beers galore.
LA1 1SU T:01524 63828

Vine Inn, Kinver
WHY?
Enville & Kinver ales, huge beer garden & walk to Hyde Lock.
DY7 6LJ T:01384 877291

The Wheelhouse, Falkirk
WHY?
Falkirk Wheel.
FK1 4AD T:01324 673490

Your local pub
WHY?
Support your local. The canals are riddled with pubs. Hundreds more..

More pubs on
www.coolcanalsguides.com

BREWING
P.T.O.
PUB'S
IS WAY
BLACK COUNTRY ALES
PIG on the WALL
visit your next pu
by boat
DEN'S
COUNTRY
BLACK BUTTE PORTER
AFRAID YOU MIGHT TASTE SOMETHING LAGERBOY?
RIDLEY'S
OLD BOB
MARSTON'S
OLD EMPIRE
LLER'S
Refreshing
SUMME
ALE
www.bathams.co.uk

Tastes Light

Hobsons
BREWERY
Tel: 01299 270837

get
OUTDOORS
and
DIRTY

AK
CASK CONDITIONED
BITTER

Purity

WING

FULL
ES

Champion

YOUNG'S

PINT

Gone gongoozling

On a pub day out, you might explore the marvels of waterways engineering, visit a heritage site, see rare species of wildlife, go for a waterside amble or just feed the ducks. But every canal pub day out really is about 'gongoozling'.

So what is a gongoozler?

It's a word that belongs to the canals, but the popular definition says it's 'an idle spectator'. No doubt, in past times, when the canals were industrious trade routes travelled by hard-working boat families, 'idle' would have been a damning accusation... but on this millenium's waterways, 'idle' has become a respectable purpose.

Canals are about idle days messing about in boats, or the more cheeky but ultimate idleness of watching other people messing around in boats! Gongoozling is the latter.

In any ordinary street in Britain it wouldn't be polite to stand and stare at someone trying to manoeuvre their car into a tight parking slot, or steer round a tight bend, or wait in a queue at the traffic lights - but on the water road, it's expected.

Anyone who goes to the canals can't help but become a gongoozler. It's the nature of the beast to want to watch the activities of boats on the water. We're impressed by eccentrics, snazzy dressers, crews with slick skills and exceptional tillerwork. And human nature can't help tittering at a boater's mistake or a bump or scratch.

It's usually boaters who label landlubbed onlookers 'gongoozlers'. Generally no insult is intended, but it does come with a glint in the boater's eye. Gongoozlers are either a shy boater's nightmare or the proud helmsman's chance to show off: nothing exists in between.

How can you go gongoozling?

Cyclists and walkers slow down to watch, and others simply arrive at the canalside with a flask and a deckchair. Do either of these, and you're a gongoozler, but surely the best way is to bag a prime seat in the beer garden of a canal pub, and watch the water world go by.

Where did the word come from?

One theory is that it comes from the Linconshire slang/dialect 'gawn' and 'gooze', meaning stare or gape. No one really knows the true origins, but its use has spread since the waterways became popular after the 1970s.

Things to look out for

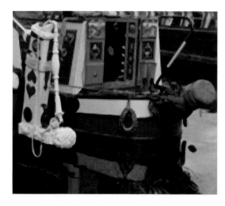

Wildlife

Canals are a haven for wildlife - a network of green corridors criss-cross the land with miles of hedgerows, trees, flowers and grasses. There are over 1,000 wildlife conservation sites and 65 Sites of Special Scientific Interest (SSSIs) along the canals.

Otters, kingfishers, ducks, swans, geese, moorhens, coots, herons, bats, frogs, snakes, dragonflies, foxes, badgers, damselflies, water voles and of course, fish.

Walk among wildflowers and butterflies on the water's edge. Tiptoe onto the towpaths at dawn and watch water life secretly waking, or go at dusk and you could bump into a bat or two under the bridges and trees.

To find your nearest canal, visit www.waterscape.com

Traditional narrowboats

Signwritten and decorated in the traditional colours of the canals...and adorned with beautifully functional rope fenders and knotwork, lacework and brass...

Roses & Castles

The traditional folk art of working boat families. A boatman's cabin and its paraphernalia would have been crudely daubed with brightly-coloured roses and castles. Canal folk art is still alive today, decorating pots and pans, planks and poles, and even souvenirs you can buy.

Dogs in traditional boat bandanas

Some are on holiday, and some live aboard narrowboat homes. And while waggy tails get all the fuss, there might be a quiet boat cat snoozing on the decks.

Mileposts

Every canal company had its own style of mileposts, lock numbers and lock name posts. Spot a milepost and the Industrial Revolution is looking you straight in the eye. The canals, built under Acts of Parliament, were required to have mileposts showing the working boatmen how far they had travelled and therefore how much they had to pay the canal companies who charged on a tonne and mile basis.

The mileposts' story doesn't stop with the Victorians; it goes on into World War II, telling the signspotter secret tales of national security. Many milestones were removed to prevent Nazi invaders mapping the country easily. Those signs that weren't lost or melted down for the war effort were put back after the war. But many had to wait years before local canal societies raised enough funds to replace them. To avoid confusion, new replica replacements are usually slightly altered from the originals.

Plaques

When you see a large collection of
brass plaques, displayed on the back
doors of a narrowboat, you'll know that
the helmsman is well-travelled.
Individual canals have their own
emblem on a small brass plaque
that boaters can collect once they've
cruised a canal.

Hidden history

Aqueducts, tunnels and fancy
engineering marvels are the obvious
attractions for sightseers. But those
who know where to look, will discover
a historic story accidently written
into the landscape by the daily life
of ordinary boat families. If you look
closely at the bricks on the underside
of bridges, or the stonework on lock
sides, you'll sometimes see gauged
marks from the ropes that horses once
towed heavy boats laden with cargo
by. Some of the grooves are so deep
you can run your fingers through and
feel the daily sweat of those horses.
There's something very special about
touching history so intimately.

Stone masons' signatures

In the stonework of the canals, on
aqueducts and bridges, you can
sometimes see the signature of a
stone mason if you look closely.

Datestones

Often secluded in the brickwork of
canal structures.

Locks

Lock arms are painted in the uniform
(and utterly seductive) black and
white colours of British Waterways.
They stretch out across the water
giving Britain's canals their unique
landscape. Some lock arms are metal
but probably the most beautiful are
wooden. Locks are operated simply by
opening and shutting paddles at either
end of a chamber to let water in or out.

How a lock works

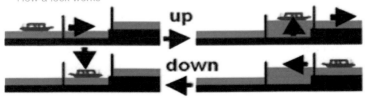

The 7 Wonders of the Waterways

Robert Aickman, founder of the Inland Waterways' Association (IWA), drew up a list over fifty years ago of some of the most amazing canal engineering feats:

Pontcysyllte Aqueduct

See narrowboats fly through sky on UK's highest aqueduct, 127ft over River Dee.
Details: Pontcysyllte Aqueduct
Location: Trevor Basin
Llangollen Canal OS SJ270420
Further info: A World Heritage Site.
Pub: Telford Inn (see pg 137).

Standedge Tunnel

3¼ mile-long tunnel through the Pennines, as if they weren't in the way at all.
Details: Standedge Tunnel & Visitor Centre T:01484 844298 www.standedge.co.uk
Location: Marsden
Huddersfield Narrow Canal OS SE040120
Further info: Open April-Oct. Visitor Centre with café, guided & through boat trips.
Pub: Tunnel End Inn (see pg 49).

Burnley Embankment

The 'straight mile' carries the canal over Burnley's rooftops, near Weavers' Triangle.
Details: Burnley Embankment
Location: Burnley
Leeds & Liverpool Canal OS SD844325
Further info: Almost a mile long and up to 60ft high in places.
Pub: Inn on the Wharf T:01282 459951

Barton Swing Aqueduct

A canal full of water amazingly swings out of the way for ships on the canal below.
Details: Barton Swing Aqueduct
Carries the Bridgewater Canal over the Manchester Ship Canal.
Location: Barton upon Irwell
Bridgewater Canal OS SJ767976
Further info: Operates all year.
Pub: Packet House T:0161 7890047

Bingley 5 Rise

Unique 5-lock staircase to heaven carries the canal up 60ft above Bingley's mills.
Details: Bingley Five Rise T:0113 2816860
Location: Bingley
Leeds & Liverpool Canal OS SE107399
Further info: Boat passage to be booked.
Pub: Ferrands Arms T:01274 563949

Caen Hill Flight

16 wide locks pounded closely together take boats miraculously up and down hill.
Details: Caen Hill Flight
Location: Devizes.
Kennet & Avon Canal OS ST983614
Further info: Highlight of 29 locks in the 2¼ miles leading to Devizes.
Pub: Three Magpies T:01380 828389

Anderton Boat Lift

The 'cathedral' of the canals lifts boats from the Trent & Mersey Canal to the Weaver.
Details: Anderton Boat Lift
T:01606 786777 www.andertonboatlift.co.uk
Location: Anderton, Northwich. Trent & Mersey Canal/Weaver Nav OS SJ647753
Further info: Visitor Centre open from February, boat lift and river trips Mar-Oct.
Pub: Stanley Arms T:01606 75059

The Falkirk Wheel

(Not in the original list - a new 8th wonder?)
Opened in 2002. An incredible engineering marvel, world's first & only rotating boat lift.
Details: Falkirk Wheel
T:08700 500208 www.thefalkirkwheel.co.uk
Location: Falkirk
Union/Forth & Clyde Canals OS NS852801
Further info: Lifts boats 115ft.
Pub: The Wheelhouse T:01324 673490

Waterways Who's Who

The great engineers

James Brindley (1716-1772)
Pioneering genius responsible for the first canals and for developing the concept of canal networks.

John Rennie (1761-1821)
Famous for bridges and canal engineering, such as the Dundas Aqueduct on the Kennet & Avon Canal.

Thomas Telford (1757-1834)
Prolific engineer responsible for marvels such as Pontcysyllte Aqueduct (now a World Heritage Site) and the second Harecastle Tunnel.

The great entrepreneurs

Josiah Wedgwood (1730-1795)
Founder of Wedgwood pottery, he was quick to support canal development and collaborated with Brindley on the Trent & Mersey Canal. When complete, he was able to use the canal to transport clay to his factories and finished goods to the ports.

John Cadbury (1801-1889)
One of many Quaker social reformers and businessmen who supported the canals. Cocoa beans were carried by waterway from Bristol docks to Birmingham to the famous Cadbury's chocolate factories.

Sir Titus Salt (1803-1876)
Wool baron who created Saltaire village (a World Heritage Site) for his mill workers on the Leeds & Liverpool Canal. Similar to Bournville village, built by John Cadbury's son for workers in Birmingham, both had a distinct absence of pubs due to their Quaker influence until a bar 'Don't Tell Titus' opened at Saltaire in 2007.

And today...

British Waterways (BW)
Responsible for over 2,200 miles of Britain's canals and rivers.
www.british-waterways.co.uk

Waterscape
BW's official leisure guide to canals, rivers and lakes. www.waterscape.com

Inland Waterways' Association (IWA)
Founded by Thomas Rolt and Robert Aickman in 1946. Rolt fought ceaselessly to keep the waterways open for his narrowboat Cressy and for future generations of boaters - and the work carries on vigorously today.
www.waterways.org.uk

Waterway Recovery Group (WRG)
Voluntary organisation, running work camps to help restore derelict canals.
www.wrg.org.uk

National Waterways Museums
One museum in three locations - Ellesmere Port, Gloucester and Stoke Bruerne. The museums have interactive displays, the largest collection of historic boats in the world and a Waterways Archive preserving artefacts of canal history back to the 1700s.
www.nwm.org.uk

The Canal Trusts and Societies
Tackling restoration and management of the inland waterways. Most canals have an active Trust or Society with regular events, meetings, talks and fundraising.
Why not join your local canal society?

The Waterways Trust
National charity promoting greater public enjoyment of the inland waterways.
www.thewaterwaystrust.co.uk

Useful info

Waterways

British Waterways
www.britishwaterways.co.uk

Waterscape
www.waterscape.com

The Waterways Trust
www.thewaterwaystrust.org.uk

Inland Waterways Association (IWA)
www.waterways.org.uk

Waterway Recovery Group
www.wrg.org.uk

The Horseboating Society
www.horseboatingsociety.co.uk

Waterways publications

Waterways World
www.waterwaysworld.com

Canal Boat
www.canalboat.co.uk

Towpath Talk
www.towpathtalk.co.uk

Canals & Rivers
www.canalsandrivers.co.uk

Tourist Boards

Visit Britain
www.visitbritain.com

Enjoy England
www.enjoyengland.com

Visit Scotland
www.visitscotland.com

Visit Wales
www.visitwales.com

Travel

Buses: Traveline
T:0871 2002233 www.traveline.org.uk

Trains: National Rail Enquiries
T:08457 484950 www.nationalrail.co.uk

Real Ale & pubs

Campaign for Real Ale (CAMRA)
www.camra.org.uk

Society of Independent Brewers
www.siba.co.uk

Directory of UK Real Ale Breweries
www.quaffale.org.uk

The Pub is the Hub
www.pubisthehub.org.uk

Cask Marque
www.cask-marque.co.uk

The Beer Academy
www.beeracademy.org

Beermad (beer database)
www.beermad.org.uk

Walking & outdoors

Ramblers' Association
Walking information and canal walks
www.ramblers.org.uk

Disabled Ramblers Organisation
www.disabledramblers.co.uk

Sustrans
www.sustrans.org.uk

National Trails
www.nationaltrail.co.uk

Wildlife

The Wildlife Trusts
www.wildlifetrusts.org

British Waterways Wildlife Survey
www.waterscape.com

National Swan Sanctuary
www.theswansanctuary.org.uk

Heritage

National Waterways Museum
www.nwm.org.uk

London Canal Museum
www.canalmuseum.org.uk

Canal bloggers

Granny Buttons
www.grannybuttons.com

Glossary

The canal has its own lingo...

Aqueduct: structure carrying a canal over a road, railway or river

Arm: short stretch of canal branching off from the main canal

Barge: cargo-carrying boat which is 16ft wide or more

Beam: width of a boat

Bow: front of a boat

Broad canal: canal over 7ft 6in wide

BW: British Waterways

Butty: unpowered boat towed by another boat with an engine

Canalia: gifts and crafts related to canals

Cratch: triangular structure at bow of boat

Cruiser: pleasure boat usually made of wood or fibreglass

Cruiser stern: extended external space at rear end of a narrowboat

Cut: slang for canal

Dolly: post used to tie mooring ropes round

Fender: externally hung bumper, usually made of rope, to protect hull of boat

Flight: series of locks close together

Gongoozler: Boaters' lingo describing onlookers

Gunwales: (pronounced 'gunnels') ridge to walk on along sides of a boat

Idle Women: the cheeky nickname given to the women who worked on canal boats during World War II to help the war effort. The name came from the initials 'IW' on the Inland Waterways badges they wore.

IWA: Inland Waterways' Association

Junction: where two or more canals meet

Legging: lying on top of boat and using legs on walls to push boat through tunnel

Lock: a water-holding chamber with gates and paddles to lift boats up and down hills

Milepost: short posts informing boatmen about distances travelled

Narrowboat: canal boats which are no wider than 7ft

Narrow canal: canals built for boats up to 70ft long and 7ft wide

Navvies: nickname for the navigators who dug the canals

Port: left side of boat when facing the bow

Pound: stretch of level water between locks, whether a few feet or a few miles

Roses and Castles: traditional folk art

Scumble: painting technique simulating the appearance of wood grain

Silt: mud that builds up at bottom of canal

Starboard: right side of the boat when facing the bow

Staircase locks: locks close together without pounds in between

Stern: the rear of a boat

Tiller: steering wheel of a boat, shaped like a pole

Towpath: path alongside canal built for working horses pulling boats

Tug: boat that pulls another boat

Tupperware: humorously irreverent name narrowboaters give fibreglass boats

Waterscape: the leisure website for British Waterways

Wide beam narrowboat: boat that looks like a narrowboat but is wider than 7ft 6in

Windlass: hand tool used to wind lock paddles up and down

About Coolcanals Guides

How it all began...

It's one of those dreams to desert the norm, ditch the humdrum rush of daily life...escape to the freedom of living on the water in a boat. We did it and took our 4 cats with us. We got rid of the house, car, TV, washing machine... and swapped them for a simple eco life. We hand-built the interior of our narrowboat-home using free reclaimed wood and started a new off-grid lifestyle travelling Britain's inland waterways.

Living on a narrowboat means slowing down to canal time and enjoying the basic things in life. Gathering logs for the stove, boiling the kettle from rationed water, starting the day at first light and ending it with the night's stars. It's an outdoor lifestyle where most of the good things are free and 'make do and mend' isn't drudgery. Somehow priorities change.

About Coolcanals now...

The waterways have taken us to all sorts of extremes and our travels carry on... by boat, bike and boot. We think we know some of the waterways best-kept secrets and enjoy creating books about some of the things we love the most.

Our books are the fruits of our travels around the waterways, created from our passion for the slow culture, heritage and simplicity of Britain's idyllic canals.

All our guidebooks are packed with our colourful photography and handpicked favourites from the special world of the inland waterways.

cool**canals** ●

Our other guidebooks

Cool canals The Guide
Published March 2009
ISBN 9780956069900

The complete introduction to leisure time on the canals. Everything from floating teashops to canalside festivals.

Cool canals Weekend Walks
Published March 2010
ISBN 9780956069917

Handpicked canal walks (2 to 13 miles) from all across Britain, with waterways highlights and all the essentials.

Be the first to hear about our next titles. Visit our website
www.coolcanalsguides.com for more waterways ideas and a full directory to help you plan leisure time around Britain's inland waterways.